HARD TIMES

by

DAVID C. CLARK

A personal account, for the future information of my family, which includes reminiscences of growing up on a farm in Tatamagouche, in the 1940s and 1950s, together with a smattering of family and local area history. Although intended for family, the anecdotes and history may be of interest to others.

(Written prior to the virus outbreak of 2020).

HARD TIMES

Copyright ©2019, 2020, 2021 by David C. Clark

Third edition, 2021.

ISBN: 979-8725189124

The family information and time frames for the happenings described in this narrative are a product of the author's experiences and memories of the 1940s and 1950s. A number of references are made to actual people's names and to places familiar to the author.

It is the author's hope that his memory has served him well enough, but asks that he be forgiven if discrepancies show up in the timing of any of the events mentioned.

Contact information: dherbhla@yahoo.com

Published by: David C. Clark Publishing

Printed by: Kindle Direct Publishing

AUTHOR'S FORWARD

Life during the time period from the beginning of the Great Depression to the end of World War II was very different from how we live our lives today. The early years of my childhood happened during the latter years of that period and if I don't consider the actual number of years that have passed, then those early years do not seem so long ago to me. I still hold images of many events of my childhood vividly in my mind.

As I remember back to how my family lived during the years of World War II, in the first half of the 1940s, I know that my grandchildren have no comprehension of what many people endured back then in order to provide the essentials of life for themselves. The present generation in this the second decade of the twenty-first century no longer has the knowledge, resources and life skills to subsist without any money or the current social services support networks.

My parents had to move back to the land due to the economic catastrophe of the Great Depression. I am concerned that a time could possibly come again in the future when it might be necessary to move to the farm in order to provide the necessities to survive. On the chance of something like that ever happening I feel it would be prudent to continue to maintain ownership of the farmland at Tatamagouche in our family for the years to come.

The years in the thirties and early forties were difficult times in many ways, but they were also times when we were a closer knit, considerate, ethically decent people. Although there was very little money circulating, those were times when people respected and looked out for one another. My parents enjoyed a wide circle of friends and relatives who were constantly visiting back and forth and helping one another on personal and community activities.

My family was more fortunate than many. We owned the house and farmland and were free of debt. In addition to working the farm, my father was a carpenter and had built up a small business in the village with the post office, bank and school as cash paying clients. Thus, there was a little bit of money coming in to buy any essential food and clothing needed. My parents also had a considerable amount of support from my maternal grandparents, my grandfather being a medical doctor in Annapolis Royal.

Part of my reason for writing this narrative is that perhaps I can include some information to make the next generation more aware of how people coped in the past and how they might possibly adapt to a return to the farm should that ever become necessary in the future.

Contents

Hard Times, by David C. Clark

DEDICATION

This narrative is dedicated to Olivia, Sarah, Alex and Evan. It is my wish that they will always be able to appreciate the peace, prosperity and privilege of their lives in this Canada of ours where family and friends are what truly matter.

Hard Times, by David C. Clark

CHAPTER 1 - THE FARM

I was born in 1938, and grew up on a small family farm on the north side of the Lake Road, two miles from the village of Tatamagouche. The property at that time was a bit over one hundred acres in area, bordered on the west and north by the French River and on the east by lands of David R. Bell. The farm had been owned by our branch of the Clark family, starting with my great grandfather Charles Clark, continuously since 1862.

The farm property itself has a long history. It was first settled by the Acadians at Tatamagouche in the period between 1710 and the Acadian Expulsion in 1755. The remains of old Acadian dikes on the river marsh at the back of the farm are still visible. There is also a diked pond at the northwestern curve of the marsh. The section of the main dike going east along the river appears to have been unfinished, possibly interrupted by the forced removal of the Acadians settlers in 1755.

The first Acadian occupant of the farm is thought to have been Francois Moyse, who is mentioned in various diaries and records of that era. I know the exact location of a dwelling foundation always referred to as being one of the Acadian dwellings, and I remember finding broken crockery and metal artifacts in several areas when we harrowed the field over that site. When I did some shallow digging several years ago, I encountered a row of large rocks which would have been the support foundation for the dwelling frame. These rocks are less than a foot below present ground level and appeared to be only one layer of rocks, as the dwelling would not have had a cellar. One rock in particular produced a strong reaction from the metal detector, but I do not know if it was the rock itself or possibly something buried deeper. Oral history in my family was always that this had been the location of an Acadian dwelling.

An original roadway is still visible, cut into the side of the gully to the west of the field where the dwelling foundation is located. This road, really just a cart path, leads down to what would have been the area of dryer marshland used as hayfield by the Acadians.

I also remember ploughing up broken crockery in the area of the field at the upper end of this road, perhaps indicating that there was another building location in that area. When I was a youngster there was a huge old weeping willow tree near the upper end of that road, a tree not native to that area.

The western part of the marshland itself, adjacent to the diked section of riverbank, had been subdivided into several narrow marsh lots by shallow ditches. These lots seem to be between 120 and 150 feet in width and run lengthwise in east to west lines between two marsh roads. The ditches have grown in over the years and are very difficult to find now due to the creeping vegetation. They can be seen however, from enlarged, early government aerial photos of that area.

I believe that the marshland would have been drier three centuries ago. Water levels at high tide seem to flood a greater area nowadays, possibly due to rising sea levels and land subsidence. I do have a recollection of my great uncle Henry Clark cutting marsh hay in the westernmost area of the marsh and of a small barn to store the hay located where the abovementioned old roadway meets the marshland. It seems logical that an Acadian dwelling might have been located on higher ground just up from the marshland.

There is a prominent marsh roadway running north/south through the center of the French River marsh. It is closer to the first identified dwelling location, but I have no recollection of the location where it would have made its way up the hillside.

Both possible dwelling locations lie in the northernmost, presently cultivated upland field to the south of and adjacent to the French River marshland. The easternmost known dwelling site is situated so as to have had a clear view down the French River to Campbell's Bridge and the area where the original Acadian village would have been situated. That view nowadays is obscured by trees growing along the hillside of the Wilson Brook that feeds into the marsh.

There is another area of the farm property that may have been used by the Acadians. Southerly and upstream, it is a hundred metres or so south of the southeast corner of the large intervale "island". On the east bank of the river there is a section of dike enclosing what appears to be the oval shape of a pond. There is one outlet through the dike so there is no pond now, but I wonder if this may have been created as a holding pond for fish or as some type of mill site. There is a spring just uphill from this diked area. On the hillside just to the north of it there used to be a number of Daphne bushes. Daphne is a flowering shrub said to have been brought to the area by the Acadians. Daphne blooms in the very early spring with fragrant, pinkish purple flower. The Daphne berries and the plant itself are very poisonous.

A hundred metres or so further south of this diked area there is the outline of another old cart road leading up the hillside to the field above. This old road starts from the intervale land below the spring on the lot now owned by my nephew, Phil Swansburg. The barely visible road slopes upward in a southerly direction until it hits and elbows easterly up the lane that Phil built some years ago. Phil's lane was originally the upper half of that cart road.

If one were to go due west from the old Clark farm house to the top of the hillside, there is another area of field where I have seen scattered shards of pottery. This area of detritus may have been from later settlers than the Acadians.

Directly across the Lake Road and south of our farm property was the Lombard farm property. That property was large in area, at over 170 acres, and was bounded by David R. Bell on the east and the Clark Creek and the French River on the west and south. At the southwest corner of the cultivated upland south of Lake Road, there is the imprint of another old cart road leading down the hillside to a point on the intervale at the head of the Clark Creek, the creek which passes under the first of the three bridges. The end of this cart road would have been near the location of the trail where the Acadians and early travellers from Isgonish/Masstown to Tatamagouche would have forded the French River at the head of tide. It would seem possible that this may have been part of an early road leading to the village on the south side of the French River. When I was growing up there was a farm road running west to east across the Lombard property from the general area of the upper end of the hillside cart road, running to the south of the Lombard farm buildings and crossing the Wilson Brook at a more or less level point at the south end of the deep gully part of that brook.

A possibility in my mind is that the road coming from Isgonish that would have first crossed the French River at Annie Leslie's farm would have split there, with one branch going westerly as described in old diaries as following the north side of the French River to the village, while a second road would be the one described in the foregoing paragraph to reach the part of the village located on the south side of the river mouth. In any case, this road on the Lombard property would have led to a river crossing at the head of the tide where the river could be forded. I have also seen a very old dug pit at the upper end of that intervale, just before the riverbank becomes steep, which may have been the location of one of the Acadian copper mines.

It would be interesting to have the various locations of these old workings checked out by historical or archaeological experts before knowledge of their existence is completely lost.

* * *

The next settlers began to arrive in Tatamagouche about 1772. Since this would have been only seventeen years after the expulsion of the Acadians, the land that was previously used by the Acadians would undoubtedly be more easily returned to cultivation by these new arrivals. All of the dwellings and building of the Acadians had been destroyed by Captain Willard's soldiers when Tatamagouche was the first community to experience the terrible expulsion of the Acadians then living there. These next settlers to take over the lands were brought to the area by Col. JFW DesBarres.

Col. DesBarres was a military surveyor and mapmaker who in 1765 had been granted some 20,000 acres of land (the area within the described grant boundaries was actually over 30,000 acres) surrounding Tatamagouche, in compensation for his military mapping services to the British government. In 1768, DesBarres supervised the construction of Fort Franklin, a British military fort on "Blockhouse Point", the site where the Tim Horton's Children's Camp is now located just west of Tatamagouche. When I was a youngster visiting what was then John Ferguson's farm (Bailey Ferguson's father), the surrounding moat-like ditches and the outline of the fort were still visible on the ground above the shoreline back slope. I expect that all evidence of the fort has disappeared by now through shoreline erosion and the development of the children's camp.

Old DesBarres land survey plans show "Langil" and "Tatary" as tenant names on parts of what eventually became the Clark property on the French River. The Lombard farm south of the Lake Road was part of a lot shown on the DesBarres plan as first occupied by George Matatal. DesBarres named the river the Frederick River, but that name does not appear to have stuck for very long.

These Protestant settlers were originally French speaking and suffering from religious persecution in Europe. They were brought here by DesBarres from Montbeliard, an area on the border between France and Switzerland, by way of Lunenburg, as tenant farmers to work the lands of the DesBarres estate. DesBarres himself had been a native of the Montbeliard area before joining up with the British military. For additional information on the early settlement of the area see the <u>History of Tatamagouche</u>, by Frank H. Patterson.

I have no record of whether these Montbeliard settlers ever built dwellings on the back part of the Clark property, but there is little doubt they would have taken over the areas where the earlier Acadians had cleared the upland. It would seem logical these new tenants would have taken hay off the marsh, but less believable they would have been responsible for any of the dikes or marsh road work.

* * *

The next influx of settlers to Tatamagouche came from Scotland. These immigrants too had suffered from the economic hardships of that time period in Scotland, and came to Nova Scotia with expectations of cheap land and a better life. These hardy individuals were ambitious and quickly established themselves in the village and on farms in the countryside immediately surrounding Tatamagouche.

There soon developed a major industry building wooden sailing ships along the shores of both rivers and the harbour. Remains of the Alexander Campbell ship yard can still be seen between the two bridges at the mouth of the French River.

The old growth forests outlying Tatamagouche, in what was then known as the District of Stirling, County of Colchester, were the source of plentiful lumber of excellent quality for the building of these ships, many of which were sold to buyers back in the old country. The ships would be built, loaded with lumber, or rock ballast from a sandstone quarry on the bank of the French River. This quarry was located down behind the present site of the electrical substation on the Lake Road. These ships would then be crewed by local men for the delivery voyage across the Atlantic.

In the one hundred years between 1818 and 1918, more than 260 wooden sailing ships were built on the Tatamagouche shoreline shipyards, the largest of these being the 1,000 ton "Jumma", built by D. & A. Campbell in 1872.

My ancestors, the Clarks, Coopers, Aitchesons and Johnsons came in the mid-1800s wave of immigrants, mainly from the southern part of Scotland. My great grandfather Charles Clark was born in Insch, Scotland, on November 20, 1829. In the 1841 census of Insch, Charles was listed as 12 years of age and working as an agricultural labourer. In the mid 1840s, he emigrated from Scotland with the rest of his family to Nova Scotia. They came on the ship Albion to Halifax and the family walked to Tatamagouche where two older brothers and other relatives on my great great-grandmother Cooper's side were already settled.

Charles married Margaret Aitcheson and they settled in the Lake Road/Slade Road area on land presently owned by Marguerite Clark, where he farmed and operated a blacksmith shop. It is said he attended the Methodist Church on the Lake Road, which was closer to home than the Presbyterian Church in New Annan, where he was a member. He died at the age of 94 and is buried near the front in the Bayhead cemetery.

Charles purchased our farm property on the French River, then known as the Henderson farm, in 1862, and paid $44 for it. He later passed it on to my grandfather, Alexander (Sandy) Clark.

* * *

My father, Charles Robertson Clark, along with his five sisters; Anne, Kate, Frances (Fan), Laura and Jane were all born and brought up on the farm property. My father attended school in Tatamagouche. The schoolhouse at that time was located on a lot just to the west of the present Balmoral Motel. There is an old Acadian cemetery now hidden in trees and underbrush, directly behind where the school house would have been. I remember seeing depressions on the surface of the ground which would have been the graves, when I was visiting Clayton Langille, who grew up in the house where the school would have originally stood. I also remember when I was a kid that the slate that my father had used when he went to school was tucked away on a shelf in our woodshed.

I suppose the early 1900s must have been reasonably good times and I think my father had a fair bit of freedom growing up, sort of a "free range" kid. There were by then many Clark relatives scattered from Tatamagouche to Bayhead and inland to New Annan. Dad told stories of just taking off on numerous occasions and spending a day or several days at a time visiting with a relative or friend. There was no easy means of communication back then for his parents to know where he was, until he showed up back home again. But those were different times, people knew and looked out for one another and there was little danger of a young person falling into unfamiliar hands.

My father went off to join the new Canadian Navy near the end of the First World War and he trained as a ship's carpenter on the

HMC Naval Services ship *Niobe*, in Halifax Harbour. He was on board the Niobe watching two ships, the *Imo* and the *Mont Blanc*, on fire in the harbour when the Halifax Explosion occurred. The porthole blew inward from the explosion and my father was a bloody mess from flying glass. Two thousand people were killed from that explosion. My father had scars and bits of glass in his hands and forehead for the rest of his life. I have a mangled piece of steel from the exploded ship *Mont Blanc* that he kept as a souvenir.

Sometime following the end of the war my father went to Boston to work in that city as a carpenter. Two of the Lombard brothers, Bill and Jim, our neighbours across the road, also went to Boston to work as carpenters. It was very common in those days for young people to leave Nova Scotia for work in Massachusetts. About that same time four of my father's sisters and Anne Lombard also went to Boston, to train as nurses.

I know very little about my father's life between 1918 and 1927. The 1921 Census indicates he was in Tatamagouche, but a little later in the 1920s he was working in the Needham, Massachusetts area for a house building contractor who was originally from Tatamagouche.

At some point in the mid 1920s my father moved to Philadelphia to work. There he was to meet my mother, Dorothy May Braine, another expat Nova Scotia working in that city. They were married March 12, 1927, in a small ceremony attended by other expat friends from Tatamagouche and Annapolis Royal.

Also in Philadelphia at that time was Harry Bryden and his wife Muriel. Harry had been a schoolmate friend of my father in Tatamagouche. My mother too had schoolmate friends from Annapolis Royal who were working in Philadelphia.

All this happened just prior to the beginning of the Great Depression. Soon it was impossible for my father to find work. With no prospects of work, little money remaining and no family support in Philadelphia, the only recourse was to come home to the farm in Tatamagouche. My grandparents on the Clark side, Alexander (Sandy) and Mary Jane (Johnson) Clark, were living on the farm, but were in failing health so it was natural for my father as the only son to take over the running of the farm and to look after his parents in their declining years.

In January of 1928, in Philadelphia, my father was out looking for work every day. There was very little carpentry work to be found. The outlook was dismal. My mother was pregnant with my sister. My parents corresponded with my father's sister Anne and Bill Ward who had themselves moved back in Tatamagouche by then. On January 14, with some anxiety on my mother's part, the decision was made to move to Tatamagouche. On January 18, they left North Philly Station by train to Boston, where they caught the ferry boat to Yarmouth. Then they took the DAR train to Annapolis Royal and stayed for several days with my grandparents and my mother's aunt Laura, before another train ride to Windsor, a change of trains to Truro, and an overnight at the Learmont Hotel in Truro. To complete the journey they took another train, this time the CNR to

Oxford Junction and another transfer to the "Short Line" train to Tatamagouche.

Mary Jane and Sandy died in 1931 and 1935 and are buried near the front of the Bayhead Union Church cemetery. In the newspaper obituary of July 11, 1931, it was reported that "The funeral of Alexander Clark was held on Sunday afternoon, July 5, and was one of the largest ever seen in this district. A lifelong resident of Tatamagouche, Mr. Clark was well known and highly esteemed, and friends and acquaintances gathered from far and near to pay their last tribute of respect."

Thus, I never knew my grandparents on my father's side. My grandmother Mary Jane, was the granddaughter of John Johnson, a member of the British Military who had served in Halifax on construction of the fortification of Citadel Hill. He settled on a large grant of land at Bayhead and his first son James would have been my great grandfather. One of my father's uncles was Dr. D.M. Johnson, a prominent village physician in Tatamagouche for many years around the turn of the century. My grandmother had four brothers. James settled in Malagash. Alexander married Josephine Clark, daughter of James and Jane (Cunningham) Clark of Bayhead, and they lived in New Glasgow. Brother Isaac also was a medical doctor and he moved to England. Mary Jane herself suffered from poor health in her declining years; I believe with severe dementia.

My father was always well respected in the community. He was a quiet, patient, unpretentious man, but very knowledgeable, innovative and full of common sense. He was a hard worker, but always had time to be social and was more than willing to lend a helping hand. I never saw him get angry. I am beginning to think I did not know him as well as I should have. His days were always spent on work around the farm. I had little interest in farm work, preferring when possible to stay out of sight with my nose in a book or in some activity of my own choosing. But my father made the farm into one of the more successful mixed farming operations in the area in the 1950s. Compliments were often received on how well the place looked.

At one time in the early 1940s my father was involved with other area farmers in attempting to form a Credit Union, and he also attended Jersey farmers' meetings in the area and in Truro. He was a member of the local branch of the Royal Canadian Legion, was a member and secretary of the Board of Stewards of Sharon United Church, and was a secretary of the local Beacon Hill and Millburn Mutual Telephone Company. I wish that growing up I had been alert enough to have spent more time getting to know him better.

For additional family history on the Clark side, since my great grandfather Charles Clark immigrated to Tatamagouche from Insch, Scotland, in the mid 1840s, please refer to <u>The Story of the Clarks of Insch, Scotland, and Tatamagouche, Nova Scotia</u>, a Clark family genealogy book, prepared and published by my cousins Jane Norman and Barbara Morton.

The early generations of Clarks were noted for being very frugal. Earl Lombard often jokingly stated that, "you could send a Clark up a tree in the morning and he would come down in the evening with a dollar".

George Clark, one of my great grandfather's brothers, was one of the Clark brothers who emigrated from Insch, Scotland, in the mid 1840s. This first George started out in Tatamagouche as a carpenter and furniture maker. I have in my possession an oak night table made and signed by this George Clark. George next went into business as a leading hardware merchant, building a large three-story general store on the corner where the Scotiabank now stands. George had his own schooner plying the Northumberland Strait with freight for his own store and for others. With the death of Archibald Campbell, the last of the Campbell shipbuilders in 1891, the Campbell estate was found to be insolvent. George Clark was able to purchase the shipyard, sawmill, wharf and other buildings at public auction for the sum of $80. George went on to become a member of the Nova Scotia Legislature and died in 1905 as the wealthiest and most influential man of that time in North Colchester.

One of my father's uncles, Aitcheson Clark, was a money lender, or what would now be the equivalent of a private mortgage holder. In one of the Colchester County Registry of Deeds books of his time there are many pages of entries where Aitcheson was the mortgage holder on someone's farm or woodland. Aitcheson's grandson, my second cousin, was Lorne Clarke, who eventually became Chief Justice of the Supreme Court of Nova Scotia.

* * *

Coming back to the 1930s, it was time of terrible consequences to the lives of most people as a result of the devastation of the economy across North America. But even in such desperate times during the Great Depression years it was possible for my family to subsist on the French River farm, living off what could be grown on the land and what the farm animals and poultry would provide. Most people in rural areas were in similar circumstances. There was very little money circulating, so it was common for goods and services to be bartered.

With the onset of the Great Depression began almost two decades of very hard times.

* * *

In the years during and following the Great Depression, wages were extremely low, if paid work could even be found. Pay for a full day's labour would have only been a dollar or less with usually a meal or two included. On the positive side there was no income tax, and necessities were reasonably priced. Property taxes were very low, but there was a so-called poll tax to be paid by men who did not own land. I believe that only if one paid property tax or the poll tax would one be allowed to vote. The poll tax was intended to compensate the government for the use of municipal services by those who did not pay property taxes. I also remember my father having to spend a day or so a year of statute labour working on public road maintenance, obligatory for all able-bodied men.

My sister Laurel was born in 1928, so she was ten years older than I was. She would have been born shortly after my parents had to move to the farm from Philadelphia. She would have grown up during the worst of the depression years.

Having been born in 1938, I lived throughout the time period of the Second World War. I have memories of some aspects of the lifestyle my family experienced during those war years and the years immediately following. Being a child, I was not aware of any of the hardships my parents dealt with in order to live and provide the essentials of life. Life was tough, but considering the state of the world, perhaps we were as fortunate as we could have been.

Back in those times a huge percentage of Nova Scotians lived in the countryside on small farms of less than a hundred acres in size. As an example, there were seven such small farms in the two miles between ours and the village of Tatamagouche. Virtually everyone with enough land had a garden, at least one cow for milk, and some chickens for eggs. In the early 1940s my family had a half dozen cows, two horses, a few pigs, a dozen or so hens, barn cats, and a dog. My mother planted a huge garden, which would have supplied us with all the vegetables we ate, with a few extra to sell or barter in the village.

Many people back in those times lived a very frugal existence. Thankfully, needs were minimal other than for food and shelter. Able bodied men worked their subsistence farms and, if they had access to a woodlot, would cut enough firewood to satisfy their family's annual needs. The work was labour intensive and there would be little in the way of farm machinery. Before we had a tractor, we had a single furrow plow that was pulled by a horse to plow up the garden and to plant some grain. I remember my father cutting small areas of hay with a hand scythe.

Paid work in the outside community was not easy to find. Some men might find work in the wintertime in one of the small lumbering operations in the forests between Balmoral and MacCallum's Settlement. The work was hard and the pay low but these men would stay right in the woods for weeks at a time, living in bunkhouses and having three meals a day in a camp cookhouse. The pay might be five dollars for a six-day work week, with the food and lodging provided by the sawmill operator. I have images in my memory of seeing large conical piles of sawdust along the road over the mountain from East New Annan to North River, the piles of sawdust abandoned to rot after the mill had moved to a new location.

* * *

The farmhouse at Tatamagouche was identical in style to the house in Anne of Green Gables. It was a two-story wood frame with cellar, sitting on a stone foundation. There was a kitchen with scullery and pantry, a dining room, a parlor and a den on the first floor, with the second floor having four bedrooms and a large storeroom. There was a front and a back stairway. The attic was only accessible through a hatch in the ceiling of the upper hallway, so was unused. The house had apparently been built in two stages with the east portion (containing the kitchen) having been added sometime after the main west section. I believe the age of the house would go back to the mid 1800s, and was said to have been moved from a location closer to the road early in its life while still in the smaller original section. If that were the case, then perhaps the kitchen section was first, as it would have been smaller and easier to move. I do not know which came first, only that it was built in two stages as it does have two front entrances.

My earliest memories are of being in the kitchen of the house. The kitchen was the centre of all that went on in the life of the family. Other than to sleep, most of the family's time indoors was spent in that one room. In the kitchen was an Enterprise wood stove for heat, cooking and hot water, a kitchen table and four chairs, a high chair, a laundry tub with a hand wringer, a couch, two rocking chairs, a large freestanding, cabinet style battery operated radio, a wind-up mantle clock that struck the hours, a Tatamagouche Creamery wall calendar, and a wall mounted telephone. During the war there were blackout curtains for the windows which were supposed to be closed at night so that no light would show if the enemy was to be in the area. I don't think they were ever used, although I have been told that someone in the village was appointed as an inspector. We used the old-fashioned roll-up blinds instead.

My mother had a very large wicker laundry basket, probably four feet long by almost three feet wide. This was normally stored under the kitchen table, but it also served on occasion as a playpen to keep me contained. My toys would most often be a saucepan and wooden spoon, a rubber ball or wooden building blocks my father had made.

The earliest years of my life were during the war years. These were difficult times for everyone. During the first several years of the war we were insulated from much of what was happening overseas, and life carried on in the same manner it had in the late 1930s. Our house did not have electric power or running water. The only sources of heat were from the wood stove in the kitchen and an old wood-burning furnace in the cellar. There was an old car that my father had acquired in the early 1930s, but this was unreliable and was little used after 1942 when gasoline rationing was instituted. Most trips to the village were by horse and buggy, or horse and sleigh in winter.

Wartime was a horrible time, but we were fortunate to be living on the farm in Nova Scotia. I doubt anyone really knew what was happening in Europe. Newspaper reports I suppose were the only source of information and I was too young to be exposed to them. We had an old, cabinet style, battery operated radio in the kitchen that sometimes was turned on for a few minutes at suppertime to catch the 6PM news broadcast from radio station CBA in Sackville,

New Brunswick. The radio was only on for a short time to conserve the battery. What I still remember from those news broadcasts was the reports of the ships attempting to cross the Atlantic from Halifax that had been torpedoed by the enemy, with the statistics on the loss of lives.

CHAPTER 2 - SHELTER AND FOOD

Our most basic needs in life are for shelter, clothing, food and water. We were lucky when I was growing up in that we owned the house and the farmland. It had been in the family since well before my father had been born and was completely free of debt.

The house itself was very basic in its needs. Any painting, carpentry or other maintenance was done by my father. The house did not have running water or electricity in my early years. There was a 10' by 10' concrete cistern in the cellar that collected rainwater from the roof via eves trough and drainpipe. Water for washing and laundry was drawn from this cistern by a levered hand pump at the sink in the scullery. Wastewater from the sink drained out into the yard to flow away naturally.

Drinking water came from a rock lined, hand dug well in the yard about ten feet from the back door. Water was bailed out of the well in a bucket tied to a rope let down into the well via a cranked winch in the well house. This well too was fed with rainwater from the house roof via eves trough and gutter pipe. The well was probably only ten to fifteen feet deep, and sometimes it ran out of water during stretches of weather without significant rain.

When we ran low on water my father would have to haul fresh river water from the head of tide above Donaldson's Bridge on the French River. This would involve loading an empty molasses puncheon on the wagon or sled, hauling it up to the river with the horse, and dipping water out of the river with a bucket to fill the puncheon. If it was winter, a hole had to be cut in the river ice first with an axe. Then the load of water was hauled back home and dumped in either the well or the cistern. Supplementing the water supply in this manner was a labour-intensive job, sometimes taking all day when a number of trips would be required.

The well water was cool enough in summer that milk and other perishable food could be lowered down into the well in a waterproof container and stored for short periods of time. Some people kept a live trout in their well to clean the water of insects, etc.

There was a second dug well out by the barn, which was used to supply drinking water for the animals. This well too sometimes ran low on water, especially in winter when the livestock would not have been able to drink at the natural springs in the hillside pasture. I can remember times when my father took the team of horses and bobsled to the river for a barrel of water to bring back for the cows.

Pretty much everyone during those times had a dug well, or possibly a spring, as their primary source of water. The Lombards across the road from us did not have a good well so besides their cistern in the cellar they had a large rain barrel by the back door to collect "soft" rain water off the roof. Rain barrels were usually old molasses puncheons made of wooden staves with metal or thin wooden bands wrapped around to hold them together. These puncheons would be two to three times the size of a present 45-gallon steel drum.

No running water in the house meant there was no bathroom. Instead there was an outhouse, "the backhouse", located out behind the woodshed. This was used only during the warmer seasons of the year. The rest of the year there were chamber pots stored in commodes in the bedrooms or under the beds. These would be dumped daily into a slop pail which was emptied onto the animal manure pile behind the barn.

The outhouse would have been stocked with an ample supply of newspapers, as toilet paper was either not available or an unaffordable luxury. I also remember that old Eaton's and Simpson's catalogues were to be found in the outhouse, but they may have been more for their visual content than for practical use. The stiff paper used for catalogue pages provided less than satisfactory results.

The bedroom commode cabinets also had a ceramic basin and pitcher for water. Face cloths and hand towels hung within reach. Full baths were once a week or longer apart using the big galvanized laundry tub placed on the kitchen floor. After supper on Saturday night, a wash boiler of water would be placed on the two front burners of the wood stove then heated for the bathwater. Once heated, the water was dipped out and into the tub as required. Baths would be taken in order of lowest seniority.

The house was built of wood, sided with wooden shingles on the outside, and had lathe and plaster walls on the inside. I do not believe the walls had any insulation, for the cold in winter seemed to seep right through. The windows were single pane glass, but my father's annual ritual would be to install storm windows on the outside in the fall and then remove them again in the spring.

I still shiver to think how cold the house was in winter, except in the kitchen with the heat from the wood stove. There was a wood furnace in the cellar, but that was only used in winter if there was company visiting. The rest of the time the main west part of the house was closed off and we only used the part with the kitchen and the two bedrooms above.

Fire was always a concern. The kitchen stove burned wood. It had a stove pipe that came straight up from the back of the stove to an elbow, then a sloped section of pipe to where the pipe entered through the plaster wall into the brick chimney. Burning so much wood meant that soot and creosote collected over time in the stovepipe and the chimney itself. It was an annual event to take the stovepipes down and clean out the accumulated soot.

There were times with a really hot fire in the stove that there was a chance the creosote in the brick chimney might also catch fire. This was a very worrisome event because there was always the danger that if the chimney got too hot then the wooden walls surrounding it might also catch fire. The quick action if ever there was a chimney fire was to throw a package of baking soda on the fire in the stove firebox and extinguish it quickly. Then wait and see if the fire in the chimney would burn itself out quickly or if a call for help would be needed.

Most people had their chimneys cleaned on a regular basis. This job required being able to get up on the roof of the house to access the top of the chimney and also to have a cleanout port at the base of the chimney. The chimney cleaning device was usually a small, bushy young spruce tree, which was attached to a wire dropped down through the inside of the chimney from the roof. The spruce tree was then stuffed in through the cleanout port and pulled upward through the chimney to the roof. If the spruce was bristly enough it acted as a brush to loosen the soot, which would then fall back down to be scooped out through the cleanout. Most houses had a permanent ladder on the roof just to access the top of the chimney.

I slept on a straw mattress, first in an iron crib painted white with lead paint, then on a single cot at the top of the back stairs. The mattress was really just a big cloth bag, probably made from a folded over bed sheet, with the straw changed for fresh each fall.

Hot water bottles were a popular addition to any bed on cold winter nights. The ones I remember were like a rubber pouch, brown or red in colour, rectangular, about a foot long by ten inches wide by an inch and a half thick, and had a screw type stopper to allow the pouch to be filled. Before bedtime, water would be heated almost to boiling in the stovetop teakettle, then the hot water bottle would be filled and the stopper tightened in place. The hot water bottle would be taken to bed and used to keep one's feet warm as we dropped off to sleep. Sometimes used as an alternative would be a clay brick or a flat piece of rock, which would be heated on the stove top and wrapped in a towel to take into bed.

I believe that temperatures were more extreme seventy-five or more years ago. This was certainly the case at the farm in Tatamagouche, especially in comparison to Truro where the temperatures are more moderate due to tidal actions of the Bay of Fundy. In my mother's diaries from the late 1930s it was common for her to mention winter temperatures of more than twenty degrees below zero Fahrenheit. Similarly, in summer she might mention temperatures of 90 degrees (Fahrenheit) in the shade.

I still remember the moaning of the wind on a cold winter night and of waking in the morning to scrape a quarter inch of frost off the inside of a window pane to see outside. One of the vows I made when I left home as an adult was that any home of mine would be kept warm so that I would never be cold in that same way again.

I have been told that some older houses in the village have walls insulated with silica flour. Silica flour is actually Diatomaceous Earth, the fossilized shells of a prehistoric, silica-based entity that flourished in several freshwater lakes in the Cobequid Highlands. At one time in the 1940s there was a silica recovery plant operating at the top of the hill just north of Rhude's Pond. The diatomaceous earth was quarried as a layer of grey muck from the lake bottom and transported by tramway to be dried in a wood fired kiln. The kiln-dried product ended up as a very fine, very lightweight, white powder. It would also have been used as a base for polishing powder, paint and who knows what else. I hold a vivid image in my memory as a child of seeing the kiln in operation, with the bright flame of the fire in the kiln and a group of men working the plant to produce and bag up the silica flour. I believe that Mr. Ray Donaldson, who lived in Tatamagouche, was the manager of the production operation.

* * *

I do not remember ever being hungry. A benefit of living on a farm was that there was always something that could be eaten to keep the hunger pangs at bay. There certainly were times when what was on my plate did not appeal, but I am sure it would have been good nutritious food. I do remember occasions when my mother did not seem to have a lot of food on her plate but perhaps that was only a matter of how she divvied up the meal as my father had a very healthy appetite.

There was always a huge garden in summer and we grew all of the vegetables we ate throughout the year. There would be rows and rows of potatoes, which would be dug in September and stored in old burlap, cattle feed bags in the coldest part of the house cellar. The harvest would probably have been ten to fifteen of these hundred-pound bags. There would still be enough potatoes left in the spring to use as seed for the next year's crop. Turnips, carrots, and cabbage were the other vegetables that would keep for a long time if stored in the cellar. A version of colcannon (potato, cabbage, onion, turnip) was a winter dish my mother used to make. Winter squash and onions also lasted for months, but they were stored up on the bedroom floor where the air was dryer. Parsnips were left in the ground in the fall and when there was a January thaw or when the frost came out in early spring the parsnips could be dug fresh and eaten during those off-season months. Brussell sprouts were left on the plant stalks in the fall and could be picked frozen during the winter.

Dinner, our big meal of the day, was always at noon. Then there would be leftovers made into hash, or sometimes poached eggs at suppertime. We ate a lot of vegetable hash. Perhaps that is why turnips, cabbage and parsnips are not my favorite vegetables.

Summer vegetables were peas planted every two weeks from May onward, green and yellow beans, broccoli, cauliflower, tomatoes, peppers, lettuce, cucumbers, beets, Swiss chard, spinach, and corn.

A row or two of winter beans would be planted in the garden and left to ripen. Once the seed pods had ripened, they would be picked and taken into the kitchen to dry out in a large cardboard box by the wood stove. One of our chores when we had idle time would be to shell these bean pods and store the beans dry in quart glass jars, to be available to use during the winter for baked bean and homemade brown bread suppers on Saturday nights.

There was a small orchard in the area behind the house and barn. In addition to apple trees there were single plum, cherry, and pear trees. None of the fruit trees produced well except for the "Yellow Transparent" apple tree. The apples of the Yellow Transparent ripened in mid August and Dave Lombard and I would climb the tree to a large branch where we could sit six or eight feet above ground and treat ourselves to these apples. It was only in later years that I learned that pear and plum trees both need a second tree as a pollinator in order to produce good fruit.

During the winter there would be a large clayware crock of sauerkraut down in the cellar. That seemed to last forever.

Not all of our vegetable and fruit foods were garden raised. First thing in the spring there were dandelion greens. Sour dock (a plant which is a bit like Swiss chard) and plantain were weeds that were boiled as greens shortly after the dandelion season. In the salt marsh down along the river we picked goose tongue which was used as another boiled green. Fiddleheads would have been available along the riverbanks but were not popular until later years.

In March, with frosty nights and sunny days having a bit of warmth in them, we would tap a dozen or so maple trees. Each tree would produce a gallon or so of maple sap on a good day. This would be carted home in five-gallon milk cans and poured into the double boiler on the kitchen woodstove to boil. The sap was tasty to drink by itself. For several weeks during the time the sap was running in the maple trees the kitchen would be fogged up with the steam from the boiling sap. Once the liquid was reduced to one fortieth of its original volume it would be poured off as maple syrup and bottled in mason jars or old quart beer bottles for storage. Some of the maple syrup would be reduced to maple sugar for use on the kitchen table (and on porridge) since white sugar was rationed during the later war years and in very short supply. Sometimes for a special treat, a bit of maple syrup would be whipped up into maple cream.

The berries started in late June. My mother and the Norman cousins or neighbour Anne Lombard would tramp to the woods at the back of the Lombard farm where the wild strawberries were prolific and they would pick several quarts each in an afternoon. In August would come the raspberries, blackberries and blueberries. Wild raspberries grew in recently cut over areas of woodland, blackberries tended to grow along the shoulders of gravelled roads, and blueberries grew in burned over areas from forest fires.

A blueberry excursion would be organized in late August when someone with a car or truck, and gasoline, would round up a load of relatives and neighbours, and drive to Westchester Mountain for the day to an area where a huge forest fire had burned hundreds of acres a few years before. A truck was more popular because it would hold more people, three or four in the cab and eight to ten in the truck box in the back. Picnic lunches would be packed and the trip also became a social affair. It was a rough and dusty ride for those in the back of the truck due to the poorly maintained dirt roads. Usually though, there would be a layer of hay or straw on the floor of the truck, and maybe an old Buffalo robe over the hay to sit on. Only enough room was left for several empty five-gallon cream cans to bring back the berries. And yes, the cans would be filled with ripe berries, picked by hand, before we returned home.

Another spot my mother sometimes visited for blueberries was to the Bayhead cemetery. My Clark grandparents were buried there so we were familiar with the area. At that time the cemetery was not kept well mowed so the blueberry bushes thrived. It did embarrass my mother a bit to be picking berries within the bounds of the cemetery so I remember her cautioning us to try to make ourselves invisible by hiding behind a gravestone if a car were to pass by on the road out front.

In the fall there were lots of mushrooms in the pastures. We picked them by the basket full. They were best fried in butter and eaten along with whatever meat was available.

Fish was another staple at certain times of the year. Schools of smelts came up the French River to spawn as soon as the ice went out in the spring. We would go to Donaldson's Bridge with a long-handled dip net, and scoop out enough fish to fill a bucket. These were taken home, cleaned, rolled in flour and cooked in a buttered frying pan. I did not care for smelts as I did not like trying to pick out the bones. Trout were bigger and better, and were also in the river and brooks in the springtime. Later in the season we ate a lot of salmon. They also came up the French River to spawn. Dad and my Norman cousins would go down to the river behind the farm at night and stretch a net in the river to catch the fish. This was illegal even in those days, but it still seemed that we ate a lot of salmon.

Stored on the floor of one of the closets upstairs would be several dried salt codfish. A couple of feet long and stiff as boards, these triangular shaped fillets were very cheap to buy and after a lot of preparation could be used to make fishcakes or chowder for the occasional winter meal. In later years during my work stint on the South Coast of Newfoundland, when I saw how the cod were dried on open air fish flakes with the clouds of flies buzzing around and other creatures in close proximity, I was less enthralled with the thought of eating them, no matter how well prepared.

The fall was actually a time of plenty at home with all the food that was available. My father would shoot ducks in the marsh along the river, and partridge in the hawthorn and wild apple trees along the side hills of the riverbank. Although my father was not a deer hunter, we always had lots of deer meat supplied by cousins and from the husband of one of my mother's friends. This individual used to go deer jacking on a regular basis so that there was a continual supply of venison for his family and others. Some of the deer meat was made into mincemeat and preserved in snap-covered mason jars for use during the winter months. We ate a lot of venison. We also shot and ate pigeons from a flock that hung around the farm feeding on the grain.

My mother did up many batches of "preserves"; vegetables and fruit cooked and sealed in mason jars, which would then be stored on shelves in the cellar. She also made jams and jellies from strawberries, raspberries and chokecherries. One of my favorite preserves was crab apples. The apples were picked ripe, about an inch or so in diameter, and were cooked whole including the stems, then put into jars in sweet syrup. These were used for a favorite dessert later in the winter. They were a bit like baked apples but sweeter and juicier, almost like candy.

At some point in the early forties my mother purchased a canning machine from Tom McConnell, who lived up the Waugh's River. As I remember this was a cantankerous domestic device that never did work well and was continually being taken to someone who was mechanically inclined to see if could be made to function properly.

We ate a lot of oysters cooked in various ways. Oysters were available and safe to eat in months with an "r" in them (September through April inclusive). There were good oyster beds along the shore at my Uncle Fenton Weatherbie's farm on the shore of Tatamagouche Bay, at Barrachois. We went there at low tide and would pick these shellfish, again by the burlap bag full. They would be stored in the cold cellar and would keep for several weeks at a time. When needed, Dad would go to the cellar with an oyster knife and shell enough oysters to cook for a meal. Some of the empty shells would be hammered into small pieces and fed to the hens as a source of calcium needed for their eggs to be hard shelled.

There were clams and mussels in the French River in the section north of the marsh, but my mother did not consider that the mussels were suitable as food.

Following the war, when gasoline was not longer rationed, fishermen would travel around door to door selling their catch. Large fresh mackerel were ten cents to a quarter each. I hated the taste of mackerel as they were a very oily fish. In the spring season we would drive to Brule Shore most weekends to buy lobsters from Alfred Bell, a lobsterman there. Albert charged ten cents a pound. We would buy ten pounds of lobsters for a dollar, which would last for several meals over the following week. Eventually, I did not care much for lobster either.

In late fall or early winter when the temperatures were well below freezing, one of the pigs would be slaughtered for meat to last the winter. After the animal was butchered into roasts, hams, etc, the meat would be left outside in the cold to freeze solid overnight. Then my father would bury those frozen pieces several feet deep in one of the grain storage bins, and the meat would stay insulated and frozen until needed for use.

To make ground meat we had a hand grinder, a common kitchen utensil in those times. It attached to the edge of a table or counter with a screw clamp, and had a hand-operated crank on the back side. One- to two-inch sized chunks of meat were stuffed into a cup sized bowl on top, the crank was turned to operate an auger in the bottom, which forced the meat out through a perforated disc creating the strings of Hamburg meat. My mother mostly used this tool in the preparation of meatloaf. As I remember, her meatloaf had slices of hardboiled egg on the bottom of the pan. Another favorite meat at that time was boiled cow's tongue. It was very cheap to buy at Bill Langille's meat market.

My mother baked brown bread, using bran from one type of the commercial feed we used to feed the cattle. On special occasions she made white bread rolls. I can remember my father and me having brown bread and molasses for supper sometimes when my mother was off to one of her afternoon bridge club socials.

We always used Tatamagouche Creamery butter, which we got directly at the creamery. The cost was deducted from the monthly cream cheque for the sale of our cream. Margarine was banned from use at that time by the government to protect farmers. Even once the ban was lifted, margarine had to be white (its natural colour) so as not to be accepted as butter. Our neighbour, Earle Lombard, used to churn his own butter. He had a treadle mounted churn where the churn containing the cream was rotated by foot power.

There were several food items popular with some people that we never ate at home. One was store-bought Bologna, or baloney as it was commonly called. We had a very sick cow once, which my father was able to sell to a meat processor and was told that the animal would be used to make bologna. That ended any possibility of us ever eating that type of meat. Nor did we ever eat the other canned meats popular during the war years, with names like Spam and Klik. My mother was convinced they were horsemeat.

My mother was a hoarder in those times. Very little packaging was ever thrown away if there might be a possible use for it later. All glass bottles were saved for use to hold jams, pickles or preserves. Paper bags were saved in a pantry cupboard. The tops from soapboxes were saved for there were often contests by the soap companies where a couple of box tops could be mailed in with the answer to a skill testing question for a possible prize. After the war, when we sometimes bought dry cereal, puffed wheat came in large paper bags about two feet tall. These bags had a glass cereal bowl or another type of dish buried in the cereal as a bonus.

* * *

As mentioned earlier, water for drinking and cooking came from a dug well outdoors. But the drink for the adults would have been tea. A teakettle was always on the back of the woodstove with hot water that could be quickly brought to a boil and added to a ceramic teapot, along with the appropriate amount of loose tea. The tea would be allowed to steep for at least five minutes, and then would have been strained before being poured into teacups to drink. If the cup of tea was found to be too hot, there were certain individuals who would do what was known as "saucering." The cup would be held in one hand and the saucer in the other, and then some tea would have been poured from the cup into the saucer, swished around a bit, and then sipped directly from the saucer. I am not sure that Emily Post would have approved.

The brand of tea of course would have been Morse's. Morse's Tea was the oldest and most popular brand of tea in the Maritimes, blended in the tea store building that still stands on the waterfront in Halifax. Morse's Tea came in rectangular packages with a tinfoil wrapping, but in earlier days had come in tin cans of various shapes with different blends in varying weights.

I grew up only drinking milk and did so until years later in my adult life. One of those white enameled pitchers of milk was always on the table at mealtime to provide un-separated, unpasteurized milk, direct from the cows in the barn to a drinking glass in the house. The cows were milked by hand back then so I can even remember a time or two when I went to the stable myself and filled a glass with warm milk directly from the cow.

Naturally, we had thick Jersey cream for our oatmeal porridge every morning. Before we had a crank-operated De Laval cream separator in the barn, there was tall cylindrical can with a glass window running down the side, and a spigot at the bottom. This was called a "creamer," and would hold two or three gallons of fresh milk. When this was left to set for a number of hours, perhaps overnight, the cream would have risen naturally to the top and there would be a distinct line between the cream and the milk below. It was thus possible to open the spigot tap and drain off the "skim" milk into another container, leaving cream as the remainder.

Selling cream to the Tatamagouche Creamery to make butter was the primary source of monetary income from the farm itself at that time. I am guessing that five to ten gallons of cream per week would have been produced. From the sale of that cream, the cost of our butter, bags of bran for the cows, and the odd block of ice would be deducted by the creamery. Any money left at the end of the month went to the grocery store for essentials such as salt, tea, white flour, molasses, matches, kerosene, and tobacco.

During the latter years of the war, everyone was subject to rationing imposed by the government. I can remember once being in quite a long line of people standing outside the Menzie and Langille grocery store waiting to be issued ration books for each member of the family. A ration book had a number of pages divided into groups of perforated ration stamps, the stamps on each page being a different colour for a different commodity. Besides gasoline, the foodstuffs that would have been rationed were sugar, butter, citrus fruit, types of meat, etc. If a certain item was even available in a store for purchase, a stamp was needed in order to be eligible to buy it. Many rationed items were not available anyway, or only on special occasions.

I would not have been very old, but I still have a mental image of someone pointing out a hundred-pound bag of bulk white sugar in Lester Buckler's General store. It must have been an unusual occurrence because of the sensation it created. I remember too a glass bottle of clear liquid on our pantry shelf that my mother called saccharine, which she used as a sugar substitute. I understand the stuff is still around nowadays in powder form as the sweetener called "Sweet n' Lo".

* * *

Another government program during the war years was the sale of Victory Bonds. We did not have any money to invest in Victory Bonds, but one year, perhaps for Christmas, my grandparents gave me a brochure-like booklet to collect the Victory Bond stamps. The stamps resembled a large postage stamp and came in a twenty-five cent denomination. The spaces for stamps in the booklet when filled and held to term could be redeemed for five dollars. That seemed like a fortune then. I never did fill my booklet, but was excited to cash in my Christmas and birthday present stamps sometime after the war was over.

The Victory Bond stamps could be bought at the bank. The Bank of Nova Scotia has been in Tatamagouche for longer than I have been around. The old bank building was located where the more modern Scotiabank building stands today. Inside the old bank, the teller was enclosed in a wire mesh cage/cubicle. To do any business with the teller required passing any paperwork and money back and forth through a slot in the mesh. Sitting prominently on the counter at the right hand of the teller was a large loaded revolver.

* * *

I mentioned earlier that we did not have electric power until sometime in the early 1940s. Before that, the only light we had in the house was from two kerosene lamps. The glass lampshades would be cleaned, the lamps filled with kerosene and the wicks would be lit as soon as it was dusk in the kitchen. Any reading, knitting, mending or card games in the evenings would be done in lamplight. Dad had an outdoor kerosene lantern with a hoop type, wire carrying handle that he used in the barn to do evening chores.

Nor were there any electrical appliances that we would now consider essential. Toast was made over the open burner of the wood stove on a wire toasting rack that had a handle like a frying pan. Instead of a washing machine for laundry there was a big round galvanized washtub on a wooden stand in the kitchen. This had a wringer with a hand crank that clamped to the side of the tub. Water would have been heated in a double boiler on the stove and bailed into the washtub, one bucket at a time. I can remember my mother cutting shavings from a large bar of Sunlight Soap, to use as laundry soap in the tub. At times when the weather made it impossible to dry clothes on the outdoor clothesline strung between the house and barn, there was a short clothesline strung across the kitchen, and also one of the fan shaped drying racks on the wall behind the stove.

With all that was involved in washing clothes it tended to be a job to be done only one day a week, usually on Monday. Since everyone only had a couple of changes of everyday clothes anyway, they tended to be worn for days at a time between wash days. Washing, ironing and mending were tasks that consumed a full day or more each week.

Keeping perishable food in summer must have been a challenge for my mother, not having an ice box. Milk and some other foods could be kept in a waterproof container and lowered to float in the cool water of the well. There was also a wooden storage box attached to the outside of the pantry window that was accessed by opening the window. This was on the north side of the house and always in the shade. Foods such as eggs and butter that needed to be kept cool were stored there. Farm produced free range eggs in those times did not need to be kept in cold storage, nor did any of the fruit, vegetables and condiments we seem to automatically store in our fridges nowadays.

* * *

Clothing of course was another essential of life. I remember wearing the same things day after day. I know my mother knit wool socks and mittens for us. I probably wore wool socks in the house all the time. I do remember having a new pair of rubber boots on my fourth birthday. Gum rubbers were the standard footwear for outdoors. These had a rubber boot type bottom, came up to just above the ankle, but the front laced up like a modern work boot.

It was not until I was in school that I had leather shoes. One pair of brown leather shoes I had in mid elementary came with very durable soles. These shoes lasted for at least a couple of years until it was suddenly discovered that my feet had grown so much in them that my toes had all grown doubled under and crooked. It was another several years before all of my toes straightened up to normal again.

All men and boys wore hats or caps in those times. The hats for men would have been the Fedora style with a brim all around. Caps were usually grey wool, perhaps with a tweed design and a front beak of the same fabric.

My mother made our underwear from cloth that was available. Flour and some cattle feed used to come in fifty to hundred-pound cloth bags. These would be carefully taken apart at the seams, bleached, and then cut and sewn into underwear, pillow cases, curtains, etc. She had a treadle (foot powered) sewing machine which was essential for making clothes in those times. I seem to remember the underwear did not fit all that well.

I should limit my comments on 1940s women's wearing apparel, not having yet developed much interest at that age. I do know that the foundation garment for women was a girdle and it is hard to imagine how anyone would voluntarily subject herself to being squeezed into one of those things. The girdle had strips of thin steel sewn into it to form and compress the body underneath into the desired shape. The girdle also came with garters to hold up long beige cotton stockings. The challenge with those stockings was to ensure the seams ran in a straight line up the back of the leg. Nylon stockings were new, but virtually impossible to get because nylon was needed to make parachutes in the war effort.

Fur coats (for the women who could afford them) were the ultimate fashionable outer garment in winter. Fur coats ranged in cost depending on the type of animal fur the coat was made from. I think most coats were rabbit fur, dyed black, but the expensive ones would have increased in price incrementally through muskrat, silver fox and mink. A woman wearing a fashionable wool coat might drape a fur stole around her shoulders and have her hands enclosed in a fur muff. A muff was basically a puffy fur sleeve about a foot in length where she could insert a hand in through each end for warmth. It was held horizontally across one's middle.

In the times before my sister Laurel left home in her late teens, she kept a small locked cedar "Hope Chest", in her bedroom. This was common practice for girls in those days and was intended to contain items gathered to become part of her trousseau, the clothing, household linen and dishes, etc. that a woman would collect to take to her new home when she got married.

* * *

My grandparents on my mother's side, Dr. Lawrence B.W. and Jessie (Graham) Braine, lived in Annapolis Royal where my grandfather was a general practice medical doctor. As a doctor he had a car and un-rationed access to gasoline during the wartime, in order to make house calls to the sick in the rural areas. For everyone else, gas was strictly rationed. My grandparents did come to visit in Tatamagouche on occasion, though they sometimes travelled back and forth by train. When they did come, they always seemed to bring gifts with them like clothing and food that we would not have been able to afford to buy.

Incidentally, my cousin Anne Johnson has recently researched and put together a booklet of information on my Braine grandparents.

There is quite a bit of family history available on the Braine side of the family. Some family member did searches going back to the time of the reign of Queen Anne when one of my Braine ancestors was physician to the Queen. My Braine great grandfather, Robert Thomas Braine, was manager of the Merchants Bank of Halifax, which in later years became the Royal Bank of Canada. His wife, my great grandmother, was Eliza Anne Buckley, closely related to the Buckley's cough syrup founder. I am in possession of the set of silver flatware that was used by my great grandparents for entertaining at dinner parties as part of Halifax high society in those times. Also still in the family are a mahogany sideboard and mahogany hall table. These pieces go back a couple of generations earlier and came to Nova Scotia at the time of the arrival of United Empire Loyalists from New York to Shelburne.

Life in Halifax in the late 1800s, for my maternal grandparents' family, would have been like another world in comparison to the lifestyle of my paternal grandparents' family on the farm in Tatamagouche. Both grandfathers were highly respected men in their own communities, but the lifestyles of their families differed widely.

It is said that my grandfather Braine and his siblings lived much the way one would read about in an English historical novel. The siblings growing up would have been raised under the tutelage of a hired governess and they would have spent much of their time on the second floor or in the back garden of their large house at 124 Tower Road, Halifax. They only ate downstairs once a week with their father on Sunday night, dressed I am sure in their fashionable clothes and on their very best behavior.

There is an interesting family anecdote on how my grandfather came to study medicine and become a GP (General Practitioner) doctor. It seems that his sister, my great aunt Winifred, had her heart set on becoming a doctor, but in Victorian era Halifax with its social climate of male dominance this was next to impossible. My great grandfather decreed that the only way she could enter Dalhousie medical school was if her brother also attended with her. Thus it was that the two siblings studied together and both became medical doctors, with Winifred being one of the first woman doctors to graduate from Dalhousie University in the late 1890s.

My grandfather's other siblings also had successful life experiences. One brother became a druggist and two sisters were governesses, one for a Prince of Belgium and one in the service of the British royal family.

(For more information please refer to the book <u>Petticoat Doctors</u>, by Enid MacLeod.)

CHAPTER 3 - TRANSPORTATION

The common way to travel any distance during the war years was by train. In times past, Nova Scotia had an extensive railway system which served the population well in the transportation of people and goods to most parts of the Province. There was twice daily CNR passenger service through Tatamagouche to Oxford Junction or to Stellarton, where one could change trains to go to Truro, Moncton or Cape Breton. The rail line from Oxford to Stellarton through Tatamagouche was known as the "Short Line." It was an alternate route to the main line that passed over the Cobequid Hills to Truro, and thence on to Cape Breton. These trains through Tatamagouche, with their coal fired engines, hauled both passengers and freight. There would be at least one passenger car, freight cars, a mail car and a caboose. In later days the passenger service degenerated to a rail liner that was locally nicknamed "the jitney".

It was an exciting time to be at the railway station for the arrival of a train. There was lots of activity with passengers milling around while luggage, freight and canvas sacks of mail were transferred from the baggage car to the wagon-style trolleys for transfer into and out of the station. The railway station was really the hub of the village at train times. The mail and most freight came and went by train. Mr. Robert Colburne was the stationmaster.

Just to the west of the station was located a water tower where the steam locomotive engines could replenish their water supply.

There was also a wooden rail and post stockyard close to the bottom of the station road just south of the station itself. This stockyard was where pigs or cattle could be brought by local farmers prior to shipment to Moncton for slaughter. The pigs would be tattooed, and then loaded onto railcars for shipment. My uncle, Fenton Weatherby, was the local coordinator at the stockyard. Later on, his duties were passed over to his son Donald.

When my sister Laurel went "in training" to be a nurse at the Victoria General Hospital in Halifax, she travelled by train from Tatamagouche. I have travelled by train from Tatamagouche to Annapolis Royal, by changing trains at Oxford Junction, Truro and Windsor.

I do have a memory of going to Halifax at some point in time during the war years, either in my grandparents' car or by train. The image I have is of travelling along the shore of Bedford Basin near the Moir's Chocolate factory and seeing all the warships and freighters, probably fifty or more, anchored in the Basin waiting to sail out on a convoy to Europe. Ships loaded with soldiers, war supplies and other provisions heading to Great Britain had to travel in convoys, with navy ships surrounding the convoy group to protect it from Nazi submarines. The enemy submarines would attempt to torpedo any stragglers.

During that time period we also used to see a large number of army vehicles and soldiers in uniform in and about the Tatamagouche area. The Debert army base during wartime held a fluctuating population of some 30,000 military personnel, and Tatamagouche was close enough that there would often be training exercises near the village with fleets of vehicles and wheel mounted artillery guns. On one such maneuver, there were ten or more army trucks and a hundred or more soldiers stopped for lunch in our intervale field by the first bridge at Donaldson's on the French River.

* * *

A couple of times during the early 1940s my mother and I travelled by train to Annapolis Royal to spend a week or so visiting with my grandparents. My grandparents at that time lived in what they called "the Cabin", on the South Mountain hillside south of the Dugway Road near the three bridges at Laquille. The property was forested and the water system for the house was gravity fed from a spring further up the hillside.

My grandfather was a GP doctor and much of his practice included making house calls to the sick in the areas surrounding Annapolis, from Round Hill to Clementsport, and from Upper Granville to Karsdale and Parker's Cove. Because of this he was not subject to wartime gas rationing for his car. My grandmother, my mother and I would often go along on these house calls just for a drive in the car. My memory of these outings was of being bored as we were cooped up in the car waiting for what seemed to me like hours while my grandfather tended to his patients in their homes.

On one of the car trips with my grandparents, we travelled the main highway through the area to the west of the town of Digby. I distinctly remember passing by a roadside fence where were hung a number of colourful paintings with a sign in bold letters that they were sale for $1.00 and $2.00 each. I remember that I expressed some curiosity and my grandmother scoffed that they were hand done and very crude and not worth the money. Little did anyone envisage what one of those Maud Lewis originals would be worth in the future.

The train ride back from Annapolis to Truro via the DAR was also a tiresome trip for me. This train made many stops along the way for passengers, freight, and perhaps even milk and farm produce to bring to Truro. There would have been a change of trains in Windsor as the line split there with one leg going on to Bedford and ours to Truro.

* * *

I have recently learned from Terry White that back in the very early 1900s there was a proposal to build a railway line from Brule to Truro, as at that time there was a ferry operating from the Brule wharf to Charlottetown, Prince Edward Island. Sybil Henderson Crawford has provided me with a link to the group picture of the survey crew led by her grandfather, E.L.W. Haskett-Smith, an engineer and surveyor who organized the actual route survey. Along with their surveying equipment this 1902 picture included the following crew members: John Warwick, George Bassy, Herbert Terry, King Langille, Bob Bell, George Matheson, George MacMillan, John Murdock, John Reid, George Swan, Truman MacLellan, George Wilson, George Baxter, Frank Langan, Robert Vincent, John Wilson, and E.L.W. Haskett-Smith.

Other pictures would lead one to believe that the route under survey would have skirted Tatamagouche Mountain and have passed through the Earltown area. Obviously, this railway line proposal never came to fruition, but it is an interesting bit of historical information that is all but forgotten now.

* * *

In the early forties of the war years there was a period of time when the living conditions for my family had improved somewhat. My father had built up a small carpentry business in the village with the school, bank, and post office as occasional clients. Thus there was a bit of money coming in to buy necessities and to operate the car. The car was a 1935 Pontiac bought second hand from Arnold MacLennan in 1942, and it was used to go back and forth to the village when road conditions were favourable. My mother could drive, so she was able to use the car to call on friends for tea and attend social events in the village. Unfortunately, gasoline also became rationed in 1942, as a result of the war effort. The car was then forced to sit idle in the barn except for rare occasions.

My sister usually walked back and forth the two miles to school with the Norman girls. In spring and early winter when the dirt roads were difficult, it was common for our family to walk to church or to events in the village. Sometimes it was possible to catch a ride with a neighbour. My mother's friends' husbands were good about coming to pick her up and drive her back home again after bridge parties, etc. All of the country roads in those times were dirt surfaced with patches of light gravel few and far between. Thus it was that with a prolonged thaw in winter or when the frost came out of the ground in the spring, the road surfaces would be virtually impassible until there was a stretch of warm dry weather.

Davy Bell owned a truck with a snowplough. After a snowstorm he would sometimes plow the Lake Road between his farm and ours. Back then it might take a couple of days for the government highway plow to make it to some of the secondary roads. My father and Earle Lombard would often have to shovel snow drifts by hand in order to keep the road clear.

During the later years of the war, with gasoline rationing, our primary means of transportation at the farm was by horse drawn buggy, sleigh, wagon or bobsled. We had a sled called a "pung" that was used in winter for light duty work trips to the village, in times when the roads were snow covered. This pung had a raised buggy style seat and was pulled by a single horse. On cold days we would wrap ourselves in an old Buffalo robe to keep ourselves warm for the trip. This robe or very heavy thick blanket was actually made from Buffalo hair and had already been passed down through the family for a generation or more, probably from the time my Braine grandparents had lived in Wyoming. The horse would have had a blanket of its own for when it was standing idle while we did errands. If the trip was for most of the day some hay and a nose bag of oats would be taken along for the horse. The horse in the wintertime would have had a bobtail. The long hairs of the tail would have been tied in a short bob to prevent us from being switched by the horse when it was being harnessed.

We had a team of two horses, Belle and Molly, all the time I was growing up. I still remember that familiar smell of the horses while riding in the sleigh on a cold winter day, together with the sound of the horses' hooves and the scrape of the sled runners on the crisp snow. Although we had these two work horses all the time that I lived on the farm, I have never ridden on a horse's back in my life.

On trips to the village in the early war years the occasional "flivver" would be seen sputtering along Main Street or parked in front of one of the stores. The nickname "flivver" applied to an older model car, though usually a 1920s vintage Ford. "Jalopy" was another nickname for an older model car that had seen better days.

It would have been in the mid war years when the first tractor came to be used on the farm. It was a Ford and was bought and shared by neighbours Earl Lombard, Davy Bell and my father. That kind of ownership meant that these farms had to work together and coordinate their needs for the use of the tractor. It seemed like we "made hay" most of the summer. When making hay in the summer, the weather had to be factored in, so I guess that by the early 1950s each farm managed to get a tractor of its own. From that time forward the horses were not worked as much.

The tractor operated on "marked gas". I am not sure if was because of gas rationing in the beginning, or because of gas taxes later, but gasoline for agricultural purposes was sold tax free at a lower price. To prevent people from cheating by using agricultural gas in their cars, a dye was added to the gas by the supplier. Occasionally, a government inspector would come around to the farms to check cars to ensure they were not running on dyed or marked gas.

When travelling by car back in those days it was helpful to have someone along with some mechanical aptitude. It was always wise to bring some basic tools with perhaps a shovel and axe included. Gasoline, when it was available, was not of the consistent quality we expect nowadays. Tractors and some cars had little glass bulbs with spigots attached to the fuel lines so that water buildup in the gas could be drained off. The older model cars and tractors came with hand cranks for when the battery power was too low to turn over the starter. When that happened, it meant inserting the hand crank through a hole in the bumper into the front of the vehicle's engine and rotating the crank as quickly as possible. It took a good deal of muscle and patience to start a car with the hand crank.

Another necessary item included on a trip was an inner tube repair kit. Dirt roads were notoriously hard on tires, which were not of the best quality either. A flat tire on a lonely road meant jacking up the side of the car, removing the wheel, breaking one side of the tire away from the rim, removing the inner tube and locating the puncture in the tube. If the hole in the tube was not too extensive then it was a matter of roughing up the area around the hole with a perforated scraper from the patching kit, applying glue to the area and applying a rubber patch cut to fit over the area of the hole. Once the cement dried the tube was put back in the tire and the wheel reinstalled. Of course one also had to have a hand air pump in the car to pump up the air pressure in the tire.

* * *

At some time in the late 1930s or early 1940s and for a couple of decades thereafter, Davy Bell operated a transfer truck out of his barn on the Lake Road. The trucking business was known as D.R.Bell's Transfer or "Bell's Transfer." It hauled freight and small goods to and from Tatamagouche and New Glasgow, Truro and other points on a daily schedule. The truck was probably the three-ton style with a large wooden, covered-in truck body, so not much larger in size than a current courier truck that we see navigating our streets today. Lloyd Campbell and Warren Bell were the drivers starting in the early 1940s until Lloyd left to take over the operation of the BA service station in 1949. Warren left to drive a school bus when the high school opened. I don't remember how long the transfer operated after that. Bell's Transfer may have been replaced by Cole's Transfer, operated by Lorne Cole in later years. Cole's expanded to become one of the larger trucking companies in the province in subsequent years.

The public roads and highways in those times were gravel or dirt surfaced and poorly maintained. It was an odd occurrence when the government bulldozer towing a road scraper would make a pass over a country road. The road scraper was a four wheeled machine with a platform on the back end where the operator would stand while turning large spoked wheels to manipulate the raising and lowering of the scraper blade.

In the late 1930's the closest paved road to Tatamagouche would have been at Oxford, Pictou or Truro. During spring break up with the frost coming out of the ground most of the back-country roads would have been impassible for days on end.

* * *

I remember my father using the horses to go to the woodlot to cut firewood for the kitchen stove and the furnace. The woodlot was three miles farther up the Lake Road toward Wentworth. Dad would hitch the horses to the bobsled and sometimes I would be taken with him to the woods for the day. We took a lunch of sandwiches, glass bottles of tea and milk, and usually a couple of slices of my mother's homemade dark fruitcake. How good that cold fruitcake seemed to taste in the woods, with its almond flavoured white frosting. There would also be hay and a nosebag of oats for the horses. Lunch was a memorable experience in the crisp cold air with the smell and sounds of the horses and the smell of the freshly cut wood.

The woodlot had been granted to my great grandfather, Charles Clark, by the Crown (provincial government) sometime after he arrived in Nova Scotia from Scotland. My father was named Charles after his grandfather. Because of this my great grandfather deeded the woodlot to my father when he was just two years old. My father eventually gave the property to me. Thus, there have been only three owners, each with Charles Clark in their name over that period of almost 150 years.

My father had a sled road into the woodlot leading to an area of maple and birch hardwood. Once there, the horses would be blanketed and tethered for the day, then Dad would proceed to chop enough trees with his double bitted axe and bucksaw to make a load on the bobsled. Sometimes if the felled tree was large and inaccessible for the sled my father would have to unhitch one of the horses from the bobsled and use it to snig the tree log closer to the sled with a snig chain and log dogs. Once back to the sled he would have to maneuver the length of the hardwood log up onto the sled with a peevee. When all the wood was trimmed and loaded, we would head back home and unload the wood on a "brow" in front of the barn. Over the winter the brow would grow to about fifteen to twenty cords of wood.

Once spring came, Will Donaldson or Obed Tattrie, neighbours from across the French River, would be hired for a day to come cut up the wood. Obed had a portable wood saw and tractor. The wood saw had a three-foot diameter circular blade with sharp teeth all around its circumference, which was driven by a belt and pulleys from the PTO drive on the back of the tractor. A work crew would also be hired to come for the day to help. There would be a couple of men to carry the long sticks of wood from the brow to place on the rollers of the deck of the wood saw. There would be another man to push the stick forward on the deck the right distance to be cut into either stove or furnace wood. Obed's job would be to push the handle to move the rotating saw blade into the wood to be cut. My father's job was to catch the piece of wood as it was cut off the stick and toss it onto a growing pile of either stove wood or furnace wood. Stove wood was cut in one-foot lengths and furnace wood in two-foot lengths.

Operating the saw and chucking the wood away were dangerous tasks as the saw did not have any guards. One had to be thinking all the time so that a hand did not get in the wrong place while the saw blade was moving forward and back into the sticks of wood. I still remember the high-pitched whine of the saw blade and the smell of the fresh cut sawdust. There was no thought of hearing protectors or hard hats in those days.

On "wood saw day," my mother had to prepare and cook a noon meal and possibly supper to feed all the work crew. The usual meal in the situation of having a large work crew was to serve baked beans and fresh brown bread. Then there would be fresh warm pie for dessert. The drink of course would have been hot tea.

Over the course of the next month while the wood was still "green" my father would split each piece into the right size to fit either the stove or furnace. Splitting wood was a tedious job as it was done with a double bitted axe on a large chopping block. Mechanical wood splitters were not even thought of back then. Then the wood was re-piled or stacked in rows to dry over the early months of summer. When it was dry the stove wood then had to be moved into the woodshed by wheelbarrow and restacked inside. Once the cold wet weather arrived, wood would be brought from the woodshed into the house daily and stored in the woodbox in the scullery to be used as needed in the kitchen stove. One of my chores was to fill the woodbox every day, and to make sure there was kindling split and brought inside to use for fire starter.

The dry pile of furnace wood also had to be thrown into the cellar through an open cellar window, and then stacked again until used in the furnace for heat during the winter.

* * *

At some time in the mid 1940s, just before or at the end of the war years, we had to upgrade the furnace in the cellar. This was done by my father and Tommy Simpson, the plumber, tinsmith and all-around metal worker in Tatamagouche. Tommy had a little plumbing shop in the house at the top of the road leading up from the village wharf that I have since learned was originally a Methodist Church. I don't know how the furnace would have been paid for, other than with help from my grandparents. Or perhaps partly in vegetables and meat from the farm.

Without electricity, the furnace operated by the natural transfer of heated air when it rises. Tin ductwork led downward from cold air registers upstairs to the furnace in the cellar. The incoming cold air was then heated in a chamber over the cast iron firebox, then it rose naturally through other ductwork to the hot air registers in the rooms upstairs. Thus, the living room and dining room could be brought up to a comfortable temperature when needed. Some heat actually rose up though the upstairs hall stairway to the bedroom floor above. The furnace had no moving parts so it had no electrical requirement.

Any time heat was needed in the main part of the house, someone would have to go down in the cellar and light a fire in the furnace. Heat was regulated by throwing another stick of furnace wood on the fire and regulating the damper on the furnace door whenever the air started to cool off upstairs. I remember one particular time that I was chilled and miserable with a very nasty head cold. I sat directly over the living room register all one day, only moving when I had to go downstairs to throw another log in the furnace.

* * *

Preparation of the land for cultivation was a major component of farm work in springtime. Fields that had been plowed in late fall would have to be harrowed as soon as the earth was dry enough. We had a set of spring tooth harrows, again co-owned with Earl

Lombard, that were pulled by the team of horses and later by tractor. These harrows could be adjusted manually to dig into the plowed furrows to the desired depth. Two to three trips crisscrossing the field would be required to loosen up the earth sufficiently to be ready for seed.

Once the soil was prepared by harrowing, the next phase was the actual seeding. The seeder was a unique piece of equipment with only that one use for a few days at planting time. It was basically a two-wheeled machine about eight feet wide with two narrow trough-like compartments stretching from wheel to wheel. The seed grain was loaded into one compartment, and fertilizer into the other. A series of pipes or chutes, six inches apart across the width of the feeder, dropped the grain and the fertilizer down into narrow furrows, each created by a narrow spade attached to the bottom of each discharge chute. The feeder, like the harrows, was pulled by horses or tractor.

Besides hay for the cows and horses, the other field crops grown on the farmland were oats and barley, which were used as animal and poultry feed. Fields were rotated every three or four years; grain one year, then hay for the next two to three. Grain is an annual crop so the land had to be plowed, spread with manure, harrowed, the rocks picked, the grain seeded, and then the ground surface rolled. When the grain ripened in the fall, it was cut and bound into sheaves using an old Cockshutt Binder, the ownership of the binder again shared by several neighbours. Once bound, the sheaves had to be stooked in the fields. "Stooks" were a group of half a dozen sheaves stood upright against one another so that the grain could dry in the sun. Barley was miserable to stook because of the prickly spike attached to each grain, which scratched and made a mess of bare flesh.

The binding machine had the capability of actually tying each sheave of grain together with "binder twine" before dropping it out the back end. Binder twine was a very strong, biodegradable cord made of sisal. A roll of binder twine was a useful item to have around, even other than at harvest time. Binder twine was sort of the duct tape of those times for tying things together.

Thrashing day in the fall was sort of like woodsaw day in the spring. Johnny Ferguson and son Bailey from Bayhead owned a thrashing machine. Bailey traveled around the countryside thrashing the grain of farmers who hired him. When our turn came up, my father and Earl Lombard would organize a crew for the day and both farms would work together. The thrasher would be set up next to the barn so that the chute to blow the waste straw could be pointed directly into the "mow" or straw loft of the barn. The thrasher was powered from a tractor, again by a drive belt and pulleys. The work crews were in the fields loading the sheaves of grain on the farm wagons, and the loaded wagons were each pulled with a team of horses back to the thrasher. Each sheaf then was fed individually by a man with a pitchfork, one after another onto the feeder belt into the mouth of the thrasher. The machine did its thing separating the grain from the straw, and the grain came out a discharge chute into wooden "two bushel" containers. It was someone's job to switch containers when filled and carry the full one over to the granary to be dumped into the proper bin for either oats or barley. There would be a tally board by the bin with a lead pencil attached by a string to keep count of the number off bushels of grain harvested.

Straw blown into the barn would be used during the year for bedding for the animals. Once there was enough straw inside the barn, the thresher would be moved and the rest of the straw would be blown into a pile in the field and later burned to get rid of it. Back then, the extra straw was just a waste product.

My mother and Nellie Lombard, Earl's mother, would be working in one kitchen or the other to prepare to feed the work crew a noon meal and a supper meal.

* * *

On really hot days in summer it was always a treat to walk down over the river hillside west of the house to swim in the French River, in the area of the river bend that had a nice beach where the main river curves around the corner of the intervale island. The water was deep in that area and was warm enough to be comfortable when the tide came in over the warmed riverbed on a hot day. The hillside was all open cow pasture at that time between the area where we swam up to the highway bridge over Clark Creek. The only trees other than some alder bushes were in a patch where the spring is located. The rest of the hillside was mostly open pasture. I have coasted on my toboggan from the hayfield up top, down onto the intervale in winters when there was lots of snow.

Directly to the west of us on the opposite side of the river was an abandoned farm with a grey weatherbeaten farmhouse in plain view from our house. There was a horrible story associated with the place and people tended to avoid going anywhere near it. Some kids thought it was haunted. All I was ever told was that a murder-suicide had taken place in the house.

I have since heard more of the story. Back in the 1920s the farm was occupied by Joe Tattrie, his wife Ellie and five children. In the early morning of January 10, 1923, Joe shot his wife in the front yard, less than twenty feet from the front step of the house. Two daughters saw it happen from the doorway. Dr. Dan Murray and the village Constable were notified, but Ellie was already dead by the time they arrived. A Coroner's inquest was convened in the afternoon with my grandfather, Alexander Clark, as foreman and Jim Lombard, Earl Lombard, Will Donaldson, George Donaldson, Alva MacKinnon, and several other neighbours as jurors. Joe was found to have fired the shot and he was then held under guard overnight at the home of George MacPherson. The following day, Constable Neil MacPherson with Joe in shackles, boarded the train to Oxford Junction for transfer to Truro, for Joe to be incarcerated in the Colchester County jail. During the train ride Joe requested to go to the washroom and the Constable removed his shackles to allow this to happen. After a considerable length of time in the locked washroom and no response from Joe, the door to the washroom was forced open by the train crew. It was determined that Joe had had a straight razor secreted in the collar of his coat, and in the washroom had proceeded to cut his own throat and bleed to death in suicide.

The impact of this crime was so horrible that even the land where it happened lay vacant for many years. The house itself went unoccupied for close to fifty years, though at times people said they thought they saw lights in the windows.

* * *

An interesting anecdote from a century or so earlier concerns Robert Purves, a leading shop owner and shipbuilder of those earlier times. Robert Purves came to Tatamagouche from Pictou in about 1837 and established a store in the village. He was a shrewd businessman, very close with money, who very soon went into the shipbuilding business near the village wharf. According to Frank Patterson's listing of ships built in Tatamagouche, Robert Purves built eleven of those ships between 1839 and 1867. For a short period of this time he also operated another store in Wallace, and there built the 990 ton, full rigged ship, RETRIEVER.

It was during this time at Wallace that Purves ordered from a currency mint in England a supply of halfpenny copper coins for use at his stores. These coins had "Robert Purves - Cheap Family Store - Wallace", on one side and "Encourage Country Importers" on the other side. In order to increase his profits, Purves paid his shipbuilders with these coins, so that these hired workers could only spend their pay at his own stores.

These non-regal coins, or tokens, have since come to have numismatic value to coin collectors. These coins can now have a collectable value of twenty to fifty dollars each depending on their condition. If Purves had only known back then.

Robert Purves died in 1872 and is buried in the Tatamagouche cemetery across the street from Sharon United Church.

* * *

Back in the 1930s and early 1940s very little cash money actually changed hands. Neighbours worked together on projects where extra manpower was required. Earl Lombard, Davy Bell and my father shared the first tractor and worked together at haying, binding and threshing grain, working in the woods, woodsaw, etc. Others such as my father's brother-in-law Bill Ward and old friend Don Ross would volunteer to help in their own spare time. Nephews Francis Norman, William Ward and cousin Hallie Clark would help out when needed. I doubt they were paid very much other than in vegetables, cream, eggs and reciprocal help for their parents.

Cash as I remember was mostly coinage, and I did not see a lot of that. In the years before 1920, the Canadian one cent copper coin was larger, being approximately the diameter of a present day one dollar coin. These "big pennies" continued to circulate even into the 1940s. From 1943 to 1945 the five cent coin had a different obverse design showing Winston Churchill's "V" for Victory sign and a line of Morse Code along the inside edge that spelled out "We Win When We Work Willingly". For two of those years, due to a shortage of nickel, the five cent coin was made of a type of brass called Tombac. They were also minted to be twelve sided, rather than round, so there was less chance they would be mistaken for the one cent copper coin. The ten cent, twenty-five cent and fifty cent coins were all made of 80% silver and 20% copper. If we had been fortunate enough to tuck away any of those silver coins, they would now be worth almost twenty times their face value, just for their metal content.

Something of interest perhaps from much earlier times was the use of Communion tokens in the Presbyterian Church in Tatamagouche. Not considered currency, these coins or tokens were metal admission vouchers needed to allow a member of the congregation to participate in Holy Communion in the early Presbyterian Church. The communion service was a particularly solemn and eagerly anticipated event. In preparation for the event the Minister or a couple of senior elders of the congregation would visit around amongst their flock ahead of time to test each potential family head on their knowledge of Scripture and whether they were able to quote certain important passages of the Bible. If the person was able to answer all the questions, he was deemed worthy and was given a metal token. It was considered a huge embarrassment to fail the test. Only with this token was the recipient then eligible at the time of the Communion service to sit and be served at the Communion Table.

The Communion token used in the Tatamagouche Presbyterian Church was oval in shape, approximately the size of a quarter dollar, made of white metal and had "Tatamagouche" imprinted across one face. Eventually use of the metal tokens was replaced with paper cards. I can remember when these cards were in use in the Sharon United Communion Service.

CHAPTER 4 - COMMUNICATION

We always had a telephone at home on the farm. One of the rectangular wooden-box wall-mounted types, it had a handheld receiver, an attached mouthpiece and a crank operated bell. Operated by a six-volt dry cell battery, it hung on the wall in the kitchen. The number was 44-23, or two long rings and three short created by cranking the bell. We were on party line #44 with eleven other people who shared the same line. It was very common to catch up on the local gossip by listening in on other people's conversations.

This line and another one along the New Annan Road had been formed into a co-operative telephone company called the Beacon Hill and Milburn Mutual Telephone Company. The #44 line extended over an area of the Lake Road from the Lombard farm three miles up to the Henry Clark property, and over the full length of the Cooper Road from the Lake Road to the New Annan Road. The company worked something like a co-operative in that everyone with a telephone owned a share in the company. There would have been telephone user bills to cover the expenses for glass insulators and wire, and for the services of the operator at the village switchboard. When there were maintenance problems, a work crew of telephone owners had to be organized to go out and fix the lines.

My father was secretary treasurer of the telephone company and part of his responsibility was to maintain the books and go around to telephone owners to collect the money for expenses.

I remember times after windstorms when telephone service would be out of order for days until a crew was organized to go out to fix it. Freezing sleet storms caused the most problems. If a pole broke in a storm then someone would go to the woods and find a Juniper tree of the right size and length to cut to replace the broken one. Juniper, aka Larch or Tamarack, was always used for poles because the wood lasted longer in the elements than any other of the local softwood tree species.

It was possible to call someone else on the party line directly by cranking the right combination of long and short rings that was their number. It was common courtesy before calling to lift the receiver and ask if the line was busy to make sure no one else was using it at the same time. At certain times of the day there could be quite a wait until the line was available.

To contact someone on a different party line or to make a long-distance call, one had to go through the main switchboard at the telephone office in the village. In order to get the telephone operator or "Central", one had to push in a button on the side of the telephone and crank one long ring. When the operator came on the line the caller would verbally tell her the number or name of the person to be called and she would manually connect the two lines together through the switchboard and ring through to the right number. Placing a long-distance call was a time-consuming procedure that was rarely attempted except in urgent circumstances and over relatively short distances. Urgent long-distance messages to and from relatives in Newfoundland and the United States would always be sent by telegraph.

Telegraph was the best and most reliable means of fast communication over long distances. There was a telegraph office in a section of the railway station in the village. The telegraph transmission lines were bare steel wire lines similar to telephone lines that ran along railway rights-of-way instead of the country roads. These were also wood pole lines with cross bars at the top and the wires strung from pole to pole attached via glass or ceramic insulators to the crossbars.

I remember being at the stationmaster's wicket in the train station waiting room at different times and hearing the telegraph key rattling away in Morse code in the telegraph room. The station master had to be able to send and receive Morse code accurately and I can still see him with his finger clicking the lever on the key apparatus to transmit a message.

The common way to keep in touch with relatives and friends at a distance was by letter mail. Everyone corresponded frequently, and everyone looked forward to receiving letters with updates on the goings on of family and friends across the miles. The cost of a Canadian "King George" stamp to mail a letter was three cents.

Mail in those days was very dependable. The mail came to the village by train twice a day six days a week. We had a letter box at the post office, and it seemed there would always be a group of people milling around inside the post office at mail times waiting until the mail was sorted. Miss Etta Nelson was postmistress. The service wicket would be closed for the time it took the postmistress to sort the mail when it came from the train, and then once the wicket shutter was raised there would be a bustle of activity to open letter boxes and line up at the wicket. For people who did not have a box, their mail would be directed to general delivery and it had to be picked up at the wicket. Our address was P.O. Box 9, which we shared with the Lombards.

The first Post Office I remember was an old building located on the same spot as the present Canada Post office, diagonally across the street intersection from the Bank of Nova Scotia building, and directly across from Mr. Wm (Billy) Nelson's law office. I do not know what happened to that first building but it may have burned. Whatever happened, my father as a local carpenter was in line to construct a new post office building. He even had a set of design drawings for the new building. Plans were delayed by the war years, however, and the postal operation moved to the east half of a building occupied by Cecil Fulton's Nyall Drug store. This building was on the south side of Main Street, next door to Bill Ward's house, with Smith MacPherson's blacksmith shop up behind. This location did not last long before it too was gutted by fire, one of a couple of fires over a few years suffered by the Fulton drug store. The next post office location was in a war surplus military building moved for that purpose from Debert to Tatamagouche. It was located across the street from the Bonnyman and Bell general store, and in more recent years was used as the village museum. When the present post office was finally built, my father was passed over as builder and the contract was awarded to Austin MacBurnie, who by then was an established building contractor.

We did not have a rural route mail box at the end of our lane. I do not know why because the rural mail driver did pass by the farm every day on his route up the Lake Road. The rural mail at that time was delivered by a mail driver with a horse and buggy, and by horse drawn sleigh when the roads were snow covered. Mrs. Lombard's brother, Mr. Sherben Weatherby, was a rural mail driver I remember. One of his routes was from the post office to The Falls and Spiddle Hill, a round trip of probably fifteen miles each day for him and the horse.

I remember that we received the Family Herald by mail. It was primarily a weekly farm newspaper that came from Winnipeg and contained lots of interesting information. It also had a section for pen pal contacts with a list of people across Canada who would be interested in corresponding by mail. Having pen pals across the country was a common pastime back then and some of the friendships that developed lasted for many years. The Family Herald also ran word contests, which my mother was forever entering. Sometimes she even won a cash prize.

In later years we would have subscribed to the Truro Weekly News as it contained community social happenings from local correspondents all over the county.

Sending and receiving Christmas cards was always a highlight of the Christmas season. During the month of December in the lead up to Christmas many hours would be spent writing notes in Christmas cards to all our relatives and acquaintances near and far. This was an opportunity to send the recipients well wishes, and include updates on all the recent activities of the family. Envelopes would be addressed and stamped and a Christmas TB seal would be licked and sealed on the back side of each envelope. Christmas seals were a fundraiser of the tuberculosis association and a sheet of a hundred seals would come in early December each year with a request for a dollar donation to that organization. The mail each day was always looked forward to in anticipation of receiving and reading the annual Christmas cards with their messages. We had more than fifty people on our Christmas Card list.

And we always looked forward to the arrival of the seed catalogues early in the winter. Seeds would be ordered from the Dominion Seed Company or MacFadgen Seeds, one of which I think was located in Winnipeg. Tomatoes and peppers would be planted in April in wooden trays on the kitchen windowsills to get a head start for transplanting when the garden was ready for planting in June. My mother would first bake the earth in the oven of the kitchen stove to sterilize it before using it in the seed starter boxes.

* * *

Whenever possible when I was growing up, my maternal grandparents would come to visit for a couple of days over Christmas. Naturally, the trip to Tatamagouche would depend on the weather and the road conditions. The other constraint was whether my grandfather could get the time away from his medical practice. If one of his patients was on their deathbed, or one was very close to giving birth, then there always was a priority commitment to stay home and be available to provide medical care.

My lasting image of my grandfather is of him shaving in the morning. Before we had a bathroom in the house, he would come down to the kitchen first thing to get hot water in his shaving mug from the teakettle on the stove. A bit of soap would be added and swished around in the large mug with his shaving brush to create a suitable lather. Then he would lather up his face with the brush and proceed to shave himself with a straight razor. If the razor's sharpness was not to his liking, he would take an ordinary water glass and rub the edge of the blade back and forth around the inside of the glass.

Christmas during the war years was a much quieter affair as I remember it. On Christmas Eve day my father and my sister Laurel, or my father and I would tramp over to the cow pasture along the hillside and cut down a spruce tree of the best size and shape we could find. It would be dragged home, and stood up in an old rubber boot in a corner of the parlor. In the evening we would trim the tree with strings of garland, strings of glass beads, paper Mache bells, a few coloured glass bell, star and ball shaped ornaments, and lots and lots of tinsel made from tinfoil.

Once we got electricity, several strings of red and green Christmas lights would be draped onto the tree before anything else. The problem with those original strings was that they were only two strands of wire and when one bulb burned out, they all went out. It was an ongoing battle to find the burnt out bulb as each one in the string would have to be checked individually. One feature of these strings was that the bulbs could be replaced by what were known as "bubble lights". These were actual bulbs that were shaped like a candle with the upright narrow tube filled with a coloured liquid, which when the light string was plugged in, a series of bubbles would continually rise up the tube.

My sister and I would hang our stockings on wall hooks on either side of the kitchen wood stove Christmas Eve. My stocking back then would have been one of my father's long, knitted wool socks. On Christmas morning when we first came downstairs the stockings would be the first priority. Opening them we would usually receive a new pair of mittens, pieces of red, white and green ribbon candy and several hard, barley candy animal figures, humbugs, an assortment of unshelled nuts, and an orange in the toe. The orange was supposed to be a special treat as oranges were rationed and mostly unavailable other than at Christmastime.

Presents would be opened on Christmas morning after my father had finished the chores out in the barn. Presents would possibly have been handmade socks or mittens, handkerchiefs, soap, chocolates, ties, books, or maybe a jigsaw puzzle or a toy of some sort. One Christmas I received a birdhouse that my father had made from a wooden Tatamagouche Creamery butter box. Any early toys I remember were war-related such as soldier figures, toy army vehicles and toy guns. Gifts were wrapped in red or white tissue paper and tied with red ribbon or string.

Once, sometime after the war was over, I got a cap gun that I had been admiring and hinting for, which had been on display in the Sellrite Five and Ten for several months before Christmas. It was a Roy Rogers style revolver that took disc caps. The discs were the size of a fifty-cent piece that fit in the magazine cylinder. Each disc had six caps or shots. Then I was able to take the cap gun to school to play Cowboys and Indians at recess. How times and attitudes have changed since then.

Christmas dinner would be roast chicken; one of the roosters killed for the occasion. Turkey was not popular in those times. There would be mashed potato and gravy, mashed turnip, and glazed carrots or parsnips. Perhaps preserved green beans or beets. Dessert was apt to be squash pie, homemade fruit cake, and there would be little side dishes with nuts, homemade fudge, white peppermints and ribbon barley candy. We would usually invite my Auntie Anne and Uncle Bill Ward for dinner. Some years my grandparents were able to come from Annapolis Royal.

After the war when sugar was no longer rationed, my mother made many batches of homemade chocolate, brown sugar, or divinity fudge before Christmas, which she would package up in old chocolate boxes to sell to customers or give to relatives and friends in the village. In those years it was common to receive a box of Moirs "Pot of Gold" chocolates as a Christmas gift from my grandparents or other relatives.

My other remembrance of Christmas Day was gathering around the radio to listen to the King's message from London to the Commonwealth. Back then everyone was considered to be a British Subject, living in the "Dominion of Canada." The Union Jack was our national flag.

Sometime in the late 1940s we fell heir to one of the large wooden, cabinet style record players. It may have come from my Uncle Bob Braine as excess furniture from one of his Ministerial moves across the country. The record player could play 78, 45 and 33 1/3 RPM vinyl records. The 45 RPM records required a small red plastic insert in the centre holes to make them fit the spindle of the roundtable. I received a couple of new 45 RPM Bing Crosby records, including "Silver Bells" and "I'm Dreaming of a White Christmas", and a Don Messer record of "Lord Alexander's Reel." I almost wore these records out listening to them over the Christmas holidays.

After several days, the un-watered spruce Christmas tree would dry out and start to shed its needles. It would then be stripped of its tinsel and trimmings and thrown out. There was no special celebration of New Year's Eve until later years when people could commute easier.

It seemed that on Christmas Day and in the day or so after, there were always a few hours of free time when no work was pressing. These times, along with winter days when the roads were blocked from snow storms, or on Sundays when the only necessary chores were to look after the animals, there would be time to relax and spend a few hours on enjoyable activities. At these times my mother would set up a card table in the kitchen and spread out the pieces of a jig saw puzzle. Many hours were spent this way putting jigsaw puzzles together. We also played card games such as Canasta, Rummy, Crazy Eights and Solitaire. The only card game my very religious grandmother would play was Methodist's Whist. Any other card game was equated in her mind to gambling and as such was a sin.

The other annual religious holiday celebrated would have been Easter. Back then the school winter break was a week at Easter time. On the eve before Easter Sunday I would put out my cap on a stool in the kitchen and the Easter Bunny would come during the night and leave several coloured candy Easter eggs in a bed of shredded purple and yellow cellophane inside my cap. Later in the morning my mother would get all dressed up in her finest clothes and hat, and we would attend the Easter Sunday church service at Sharon United. The church on Easter Sunday morning would be profuse with flowers, especially with lilies placed there by the Fultons in memory of their son Cecil Junior. After the church service we would have

Easter dinner with Auntie Anne and Uncle Bill Ward either at their home or ours.

* * *

Eventually all the local independent telephone companies were taken over by the Maritime Telephone and Telegraph Company and incorporated into a province wide system. The old battery-operated telephones were replaced with dial type phones in various styles. Maritime Tel and Tel also installed a couple of phone booths in the village, making it possible for someone away from their home phone to make a private call. The cost to make a local phone call from a phone booth was a ten-cent coin.

* * *

Listening to the radio was a great source of entertainment and enjoyment after we had electricity. Besides the daytime farm broadcasts, soap operas and the music, it was the best means to keep up with national and international news. The Canadian Broadcasting Corporation was still in its early years and had developed its own news service with Lorne Greene reading the newscasts. "Hockey Night in Canada," with Foster Hewitt, became a very popular Saturday night ritual for Canadians who would not have been hockey fans otherwise.

Following the war years and once we had a movie theatre in Tatamagouche, newsreels were a popular means to catch up on the news of the world. Once the Rialto Theatre opened, each movie feature would be preceded by a five to ten minute newsreel showing a brief series of newsworthy world events, somewhat similar to our modern TV newscasts. I vaguely remember that these newsreels were sometimes shown in special gatherings at the community town hall in the years before the Rialto Theatre. Maybe they were produced by the National Film Board at that time, but the distinctive voice of the narrator became very familiar so as to always be associated in my mind with news reports.

Comedy shows were popular in those years, first on radio, then at the movie theatre and eventually in the early years of owning a television set. Red Skelton, Bob Hope, and George Burns and Gracie Allen we early radio programs. The antics of Abbot and Costello, the Three Stooges and Laurel and Hardy were all sources of laughter and entertainment at the movie theatre. Ventriloquist Edgar Bergan with his puppets Charlie McCarthy and Mortimer Snerd were always so entertaining.

* * *

Travel to any distance in those times was complicated, not so much by the means to get somewhere, as there was excellent rail service virtually everywhere, but by the cash outlay needed for the train tickets, and food and lodging. Most people simply did not have the money to travel far without stopping along the way with relatives or acquaintances for meals and a place to sleep. It was common then for anyone who did make an extended trip, say to the United States or to "Upper Canada", to drop in for overnight stops along the way with anyone with whom they might have some connection, be it a distant relative or even a friend of a friend.

Living on the farm we were tied to the care of the animals anyway so it was impossible to travel more than a day at a time without someone at home to feed the animals and milk the cows. Thus it was that our relatives usually came to us for family time together. These were the only times I was able to meet with many of my more distant relatives.

Again due to the difficulties of travel, when family and friends did come to visit they tended to spend longer periods of time. Fortunately, these visits were usually in the summertime when the garden was able to provide fruit and vegetables to feed everyone. Food itself never seemed to be a problem.

Visiting family members usually stayed for days or even a week or so at a time. Back then though, relatives, especially those coming from the United States, brought with them all sorts of packaged and canned foodstuffs that we would not have had access to otherwise. One aunt and uncle owned a laundry in Hartford and when they came to visit, they would bring a whole wardrobe of clothing that customers had abandoned over time at their laundry.

There was one time when we had a house full of family visiting that we were actually short of beds for everyone. It was decided by my parents that my father, mother, sister and I would sleep out in the barn. It was midsummer with warm temperatures so we would just take blankets and bed down in the haymow for the night. It would be an adventure. All seemed to go well at first with the smell of the fresh hay and the quiet chirping of crickets. It was not long after we had settled in, however, that a mouse ran across my mother's blanket. That ended any thoughts of a restful sleep and we were soon resettled back in the house with our blankets on the hard kitchen floor.

CHAPTER 5 - FAMILY LIFE

During the early years, immediately after my parents had to move from Philadelphia to the farm in Tatamagouche, and especially in winter, my mother's social life would have suffered greatly. My mother was a woman who always craved a social lifestyle. Having been born in Wyoming, grown up a doctor's daughter in Nova Scotia towns, attended college in Michigan, and later worked in Philadelphia, she had had a relatively privileged early life. She considered herself in the upper level of the social structure of those times. Living on a small rural farm a couple of miles from the village of Tatamagouche, with few close friends and no easy means to attend social events, would not have been an easy life for her. She would have been in her early twenties when she first found herself settled in the rural countryside caring for two unhealthy in-law parents.

By the time I came along though, and during the first of the war years, visiting back and forth with friends and relatives on a regular basis became a normal way of life for my parents. My father had acquired several customers in the village for small carpentry and handyman jobs. He did maintenance work for the post office and the Bank of Nova Scotia, so there was some cash income that began to trickle in. Gas did not become rationed until 1942, so until then my mother was able to use the old car to drive to visit friends and to attend bridge parties and other social events in the village. There were lots of Clark relatives in the area, and my parents had by then developed a wider circle of friends, so these were much happier times for her.

Back in those times people visited back and forth with neighbours and friends in order to socialize. It was a normal social practice to call on friends and acquaintances "at the drop of a hat", or in other words to just drop in to visit and stay for a cup of tea. Women got together for group events such as WMS, which was the Women's Missionary Society, the Home and School Association, and the local "Book Club". There were many evening social events such as card parties, dances, fundraising suppers, and variety concerts held in the "Town Hall", the community building across the street from Sharon United Church. This community hall was also the venue used for school concerts and other school activities.

At one particular variety concert after the war, which I attended with my parents, Ross Hamilton was a performer. Ross had been a member of the world-famous military "Dumbells" that had entertained the troops during the First World War. He had a beautiful soprano voice and as part of the theatrical group dressed up as a woman named "Margorie" to sing popular songs of the era.

Ross was born and brought up in Pugwash and lived in Brookfield in retirement, but I believe he had relatives in the Tatamagouche area.

My mother and a number of other ladies in the village belonged to "Bridge Club" in the latter part of the 1940s and into the 1950s. The bridge club had nine or ten regular members so that there would be enough women for two tables of cards allowing for the hostess and maybe a spare in case someone was unavailable to attend. The bridge club rotated to meet at each woman's home just about every week. Each bridge party required a great deal of preparation ahead of time to make all kinds of fancy sandwiches and sweets to serve along with the tea in the late afternoon. When it was her turn to entertain, my mother would spend hours in the preparation of sandwiches, Mocha cakes, pineapple squares, cherry balls and/or a variety of other fancy sweets. Sometimes there was even a full course dinner.

The bridge players were Clara Buckler (Frank), Janie Bell (Davy), Greta Bell (Warren), Jennie Fulton (Cecil), Annie Langille (Cecil), Hattie Langille (Earl), Francis White (Jimmy), Alice Langille (Roy), Helen MacKeen (Jimmy) and there may have been other members. There may even have been another bridge club in the area. Bridge was certainly a popular pastime, and there were many evening bridge parties in private homes and the town hall attended by individuals and couples.

The bridge prize for the high score at each bridge club event oftentimes was some article of kitchenware or an English bone china cup and saucer. My mother was an excellent bridge player and acquired quite a number of cups and saucers as prizes. At bridge club, the 1st prize was for the player with the highest individual score. There was also a "Booby" prize for lowest score. Sometimes there would be a prize for "lucky score card", "lucky tea cup", or what were called "travelling prizes". I'm not sure what those were.

My mother was also a quilter and hooked a number of small rugs during the war years. Perhaps there was more spare time with fewer daytime activities back then than there would be in later years. It seemed there was often a quilt mounted in a wooden quilt frame in the centre of the dining room. Oftentimes she would walk over to the neighbouring homes of Mrs. Nellie Lombard or Janie Bell or Greta Bell, to spend the afternoon helping them with a quilt and socializing. Invariably, that would mean sharing a cup of afternoon tea. It was fairly common for there to be a "Quilting" at someone's home, or even the church hall, where quilters were welcome to drop in for a few hours to work on a quilt and have a cup of tea. Some of the quiltings were intended as a fundraiser for one charity or another. Mention was made in one of my mother's diary entries for a fundraising event for Russian War Relief.

* * *

Bigoted is a very strong word and those were different times with much different cultural attitudes, but I shudder now at some of the racial and religious biases held by people in those early years. Tatamagouche was very much a WASP (White Anglo Saxon Protestant) community. Everyone was white, everyone was either

Presbyterian or United, and English was the only language ever heard. The two Protestant congregations in the village coexisted, but still with a wariness of one another as a result of church union back in the mid twenties. Non Protestants and persons of a different colour would have been looked down upon by many village residents at that time. People who were "different" were often described with demeaning comments.

One thing I was never aware of was the possibility someone might have a different sexual orientation. I remember there were a number of "old maids" and "bachelor" men in the community, but they were just accepted as being individuals who had not had the good fortune to find a suitable spouse of the opposite sex. Perhaps I was naive, but the subject never arose that there was the possibility that someone might have different sexual desires. Everyone lived their lives very privately and there was never any sex education in school or even adult conversations of a sexual nature within my hearing.

My grandmother on my mother's side was very religious. An evangelical Christian is perhaps what she would be called nowadays. Much of her thinking seemed devoted to preparation for the second coming of Jesus. When travelling by car she used to make my grandfather stop to pick up hitchhikers, and then she would give them a copy of the St. John's Gospel, and attempt to convince them that they needed to be born again. To her, the King James Version of The Bible was divinely inspired by God and every word was true as written. There was no room for any change in its interpretation. My grandfather seemed to bear all of this very stoically, never expressing his beliefs one way or another. I heard my mother comment once that he probably felt he could just ride along to heaven on his wife's coat tails.

On numerous occasions when I was alone with my grandmother, she would take it upon herself to spend ten minutes or so in her preaching mode, trying to instill her beliefs in me. Not quite hellfire and damnation, but certainly reinforcing to me what my morals and beliefs should be. It took years for me learn more reasonable interpretations of some of her convictions, and to overcome some aspects of her inhibiting teachings.

My grandmother used to suffer with terrible nightmares. It was not uncommon when she was visiting with us that the whole house would be jolted awake in the night by a series of terrified screams. There was never an explanation for why these nightmares occurred. It was not until recently, when I read an old newspaper article describing a horrific murder of one of her teenage schoolmates in Bear River, that I wondered if the nightmares might have been the after effect of this traumatic event.

My mother was much more moderate in her religious beliefs. We belonged to the Sharon United Church in the village. I don't remember attending church very often until after the War was over, but maybe I was just left home in the care of my father or sister until I was old enough to sit quietly for an hour or more. Mr. Whidden was a very popular Minister in the early 1940s.

When the Whiddens transferred to Cape Breton in 1942, a "call" was sent out to Rev. Walter Davis in LaHave, to come to be Minister at Sharon United. Mr. Davis was hired with a salary of $1,600 per year, and the use of the Manse with the promise of it being furnished by the congregation. Mr. Davis preached his first sermon on Sunday, April 19, 1942. My family attended and my mother's diary entry was that "He was good, but can't say I was overly impressed." Mr. Davis' induction as Minister had been held the previous day and my mother had also attended that service. Her diary entry for that was: "Went down to the service at night for Mr. Davis induction. It was terrible. A Dr. Betts was there and he was so dramatic I laughed so hard I got hysterical. Had a nice social afterward. Mrs. Davis has a nice face, so friendly and she looks sensible but scared to death."

When we did go to church on Sundays, we got there about forty minutes early in order to be able to sit in the back pew. I suspect this was so my mother could see how the other women were dressed in their Sunday finery as they came into the church. I was more intrigued with the cute red-headed girl who sat several pews ahead.

Although not ardent churchgoers in those early years, my family, along with everyone else in the community, did observe the religious norms of those times. Women had to wear hats to attend church. To be in church bareheaded would have been a sacrilege. If some woman visiting "from away" happened to attend a Sunday morning service without a head covering she would be viewed with suspicion. Men would wear their very best clothes to church and always be bareheaded inside the place of worship. In any home or other inside gathering for that matter, it was common courtesy for a man to remove his hat or cap. A man would tip his hat to any woman he met in passing. I cringe nowadays at males who do not have the good manners to take off their ball caps indoors, no matter where they are or what type of function they are attending.

In those years Sunday was a day of rest. No work would have been done other the essentials to care for the farm animals. For example, even if Sunday was the only sunny day of the week during haying season, the hay would have been left in the field rather than defile the religious strictures of working to bring it to the barn on the Sabbath.

I don't remember ever attending Sunday School except for one year during my high school years, when we had Dr. Charles Gass as instructor, in preparation for Confirmation. I did read in my mother's diary that I attended Sunday School several times in one of my early school years when Greta Bell was the teacher. Apparently, that did not make a lasting impression on me. I also did one year of Sunday School by correspondence under the auspices of the Ernest C. Manning organization from Alberta, which had a Sunday evening religious program for youth that was broadcast on CBC radio. There again, this program was slanted toward the religious far right and did not satisfy the want of more modern ways of thinking.

* * *

Perhaps my social life was also deprived. I did not have any social play time with anyone my own age until I started school. Even then, while in the elementary grades, I never did play with anyone else outside of school. The two mile distance and getting back and forth was too difficult. The closest friend I had in my grade at school was Ron Campbell and he lived in the village, where his father Lloyd, operated the BA Service Station. It was not until I had bought my bicycle when I was ten years old that I was able to chum around with others my own age. The only other early friend I had growing up was Dave Lombard, when he started coming from Needham, Massachusetts, to the neighboring Lombard farm in the summers.

There was a Boy Scout troop organized in the village when I was about the right age. It met one night a week in the Community Hall across from Sharon United Church. I went one night and the main activity seemed to be a very rough game of floor hockey. I never did go back. I did join an American group called the "Open Road Pioneers," which was sort of like scouting, but by correspondence. There were instructions for a number of outdoor activities and tests where I could make my way up though several levels of that organization. That was a wonderful learning experience with fun outdoor activities, but again there was no socializing with anyone else.

Perhaps from this early lack of social interaction I was always extremely shy and found it difficult to talk to anyone. I always felt at a loss for words in a situation where I was expected to take part in a conversation. My mother used to say I did not start to talk until I was nearly four years old. I know that was not true, but all through my early years I was never comfortable trying to carry on a conversation with anyone I did not know well. This shyness to talk became acutely embarrassing to me in my early teens with members of the opposite sex.

One incident in my early school years was a huge embarrassment to me. It happened in Grade 2, when the elementary grades held their annual Christmas concert in the Community Hall. The place was packed with parents and townspeople. I was assigned to be one of four of my classmates to go up on stage and recite a short Christmas poem and hold up the cardboard letters that spelled Merry Christmas. The girl beside me forgot her lines and I held up the wrong letters. I was devastated over my mistake and from that time forward was reluctant to perform in front of other people.

Having to speak in front of a class or as part of a group discussion was always reason for my stomach to become upset. In school, I always knew the answer to teacher's questions, but after being embarrassed and teased for being smart or being called "the teacher's pet," I soon learned stay out of sight and just keep quiet.

My other confidence problem was that when my second teeth came in, my jaw was very cramped. I had one front tooth that stuck out and one that went in the opposite direction. That was very embarrassing and I always tried to keep my mouth closed to hide the protruding tooth. The buck tooth was good for peeling oranges, but that hardly compensated for always being uncomfortable and self conscious at the way I thought the tooth looked.

I ended up being pretty much of a loner during my early school years and learned to keep busy with solitary interests of my own. I had a few daily chores around the farm each day, but when I was not occupied with some outdoor activity, I spent much of my time buried in a book. I loved to read almost anything I could get my hands on. After going through all the Hardy Boys and Mercer Boys series, and other boys adventure books, I moved on to mystery novels such as the Ellery Queen and Agatha Christie series, Westerns by Zane Gray, and eventually to science fiction. Whenever time permitted, I immersed myself in stories of the adventures of heroes and heroines doing all the things I imagined myself being able to do. The characters in the stories I read replaced the friendships I wished I had in real life.

All of this meant that for many years I suffered from a terrible lack of self confidence and I always hung back rather than pushing to become involved and promote myself in order to take part of activities where I really did want to participate. It was not until years later when I was in the workforce that my employer sponsored me to attend a Dale Carnegie course, and I finally gained the confidence I needed to speak on my feet.

About mid point in my later working career, after taking a personality test at the behest of my employer, it was determined that I was an extrovert. Most people would not have believed that back in my earlier years.

* * *

We did not have toothpaste in those very early years of my life. My teeth would only get brushed at bedtime and I remember putting salt or baking soda on the brush. Probably as a result of this, I had a lot of toothaches from cavities. Later, when there was more money, we had dental powder that was shaken onto the toothbrush from a can that had a saltshaker type top.

If the toothache pain was intense, I would be given a Codaphin pill. Codaphin was similar and much more potent than an Aspirin, which we never did use at home. But we did have a big bottle of these Codeine pills from my grandfather and they worked really well as painkillers, probably because of the amount of opium in them.

The closest dentist in those early days would have been in Truro or New Glasgow and that was not even considered. I did go to a Dr. Crowe in Annapolis Royal one time when I had a really horrible toothache while visiting my grandparents. Dr. Crowe put in a temporary filling using that awful tasting stuff that was used for packing in those days.

When I was in Grade 1 there was a travelling provincial dental unit in a large truck that came to the school and checked every student's teeth. Mine must have been really bad because they froze my mouth and pulled out six of my baby teeth in one session. I still have the image of the needle used in that freezing process. Thus, my early experiences with dentists did not lead me to have favourable expectations to dental visits in later life.

I understand I was a bit of a sickly kid in my early years. At one time when I was three, I was very sick with pneumonia. My mother called my grandfather to come all the way from Annapolis Royal to check on me. The odd time that I do remember having an upset stomach, the cure was worse than the sickness. My mother's antidote to any sickness was to purge the system with a dose of laxative. Castor Oil was her remedy of choice, but that eventually evolved to a patent medicine called Castoria. This was the vilest tasting stuff imaginable, with a flavour of root beer. To this day I cannot stand the taste of root beer, or of anything with that flavour.

To keep me healthy during my early elementary school years I was given a spoonful of cod liver oil each day. We kept a large bottle of the stuff at home, provided by my grandfather. Back in those days there was a health program at school whereby every student was given a cod liver oil capsule to swallow each day. My mother was able to opt me out of that program because of me having my spoonful of the liquid variety at home. I envied the other kids because they got to have the tasteless kind.

It is a wonder we did not suffer more from food poisoning due to the manner food had to be stored without refrigeration. The saving grace I am sure was that all our food was well cooked. But there was no way of ensuring that leftovers were kept at temperatures that would not allow organisms to develop. I know that bottles of jam would sometimes be opened and there would be mould under the paraffin wax. This would simply be spooned out along with another half inch or so below the surface and then the rest of the bottle would be eaten on toast as usual. Perhaps we had developed a level of immunity over time due to exposure to all those aspects of farm life.

My mother's diaries during that early 1940s time period did often mention that she or my sister or myself were sick to our stomachs for a day or so at a time. So perhaps some of those instances were food related. Dr. Dan Murray would have been our local family doctor, but in most cases my mother would contact my grandfather in Annapolis for his diagnosis first. Dr. Murray did make house calls so I do remember him coming to the house one time when I had a terrible pain in my side. It was decided though that I simply had gas rather than appendicitis, so the antidote was ginger tea.

My mother also believed that colds were caught by sitting "in a draft," or getting chilled from being wet. We were well warned about the consequences of spending time in damp drafty areas. That advice was best heeded anyway, as her antidote for a cold was another dose of castor oil.

Before bathroom scales became available it was not so easy to keep track of one's weight. Other than in the doctor's office, scales accessible to weigh oneself were few and far between. But some commercial business' had pedestal style scales where one could stand on the platform, reach forward to insert a coin in the slot and read one's weight on the needle gauge mounted at approximately chest level. The Selrite store in the village had one of these scales near the entranceway where for either a penny or a nickel it was possible to weigh oneself.

My mother was quite superstitious, but perhaps that was also a product of those times when people were less likely to question the validity of "old wives tales," or to acknowledge the simple truths that we take for granted nowadays. Some of the beliefs she held sound pretty farfetched, now that we know better. It meant seven years of bad luck to break a mirror, though not quite as long if a black cat crossed the road in front of you. The dust broom was stored behind the kitchen door, but if that broom happened to fall across the doorway it meant that company was coming to visit. One could not open an umbrella in the house or walk under a ladder as those both meant a string of bad luck. And it was wise to check the day of the week before one described a dream. My mother believed that "A Friday's night's dream on a Saturday told is sure to come true before it's old."

Each time we had a chicken dinner the "wish bone" was cleaned and put in the warming oven of the kitchen stove to dry out. Once completely dry, two people were given the chance to each make a secret wish. Then each would take one prong of the wishbone with their little finger and pull. When the bone snapped apart whoever ended up with the section with the centre piece intact was sure to have their wish granted.

A horse shoe was considered a symbol of good luck. Some people had one nailed over a doorway. There was a protocol however, in that the horseshoe had to be concave side up. While Cecil and Jennie Fulton were building their new house on Main Street, someone nailed a horseshoe wrong side up as a prank over their front door one night. This of course caused quite a kerfuffle when the Fultons discovered the devious deed. The horseshoe was taken down immediately, and the culprit went unidentified despite Cecil's best efforts to learn who did it.

* * *

Perhaps it was more of a cultural norm of earlier times but as I think back to how people behaved, I believe there was little outward show of affection between the people with whom I was familiar. I don't remember ever receiving hugs or kisses from my parents, sister or grandparents. I am sure they loved and cared for me unconditionally, but from the time I was old enough to be in school there was never any verbal declaration of affection.

Nor were the words of endearment such as dear, darling, sweetheart that are so commonly in general usage nowadays. Tallie was used by my mother and sister as a nickname for my father, and my grandmother was Mammy, but most people were only known by their Christian names. Adult men and women in the community were always addressed by anyone younger as Mr. or Mrs. whatever their surname was. Every married woman was referred to by her husband's name. If a man was describing something about his wife, she was often referred to her as, "the wife". Similarly, a youth might refer to his father as, "the old man."

The subject of sex was taboo; never mentioned in conversation. There was absolutely no sex education in the schools. Not until the 1960s did society become more open minded and conversations might include subjects of a more personal nature.

Many women in those days were stay-at-home wives and mothers, but they were not thought of as any less equal to the men who were more often the wage earners. All of the people I knew growing up were independent minded and respected whether male or female. Politeness was a given trait everywhere and all women were treated with utmost deference.

I suppose that in some ways it was still a very patriarchal society until the 1940s. I think the war years may have initiated the beginnings of change. With many of the men off to fight the war, the women left back home had to take on responsibilities that men had previously shouldered. Women took on jobs that might have been considered "men's work". I think my parents were pretty enlightened anyway for those times. I know of numerous occasions when my mother drove the tractor in the fields for planting or haying, and my father was not averse to helping out with laundry and other housework.

* * *

My Aunt Kate Norman and her daughters Katherine and Jane (my first cousins) lived in the house a quarter mile from our house on the property where Stephen Norman, Kate's grandson, now lives. At that time our farm property was larger, and my father owned the house and land where they lived. My Aunt Kate had been forced to come home from the USA before 1930, also as a result of the Depression and the loss of her husband. Being in dire straits, with four children, my father let them live in the house that had been part of the Wilson property he had bought sometime before the Depression. There was an old barn that went with the house so the Norman family had a cow and a flock of hens. Aunt Kate had been an RN in the USA and was able to pick up some private nursing work when she came to Tatamagouche. She sometimes accompanied Dr. Dan Murray on cases when he was delivering a baby. She often went for periods of time on cases where she cared for some elderly individual who was very sick or dying in their own home.

I am sure that life for the Norman family would have been disadvantaged with Aunt Kate as a single mother and not having the social programs we have today. She would have depended to some extent on assistance from her brother and her two sisters in the village.

Aunt Kate's sons, my cousins Leo and Alec Norman. were adults in the early 1940s. They joined the Armed Forces midway through the war years. Having been born in the USA, they were called to join the RCAF, but enlisted under a program for citizens of a foreign country and ended up with USA shoulder insignia on their uniforms. They both learned the electrician's trade while in the air force, so they managed to get good jobs back in Nova Scotia once the war was over.

Leo, who was then called Francis by his Tatamagouche relatives, had an old car of some make before he went into the air force. When he left home to be stationed at the RCAF air base in Summerside, PEI, he parked the car in the barn and covered it over with hay so it was well insulated and hidden from sight. Aunt Kate's chickens had the run of the barn and the outside yard. I remember helping Jane collect eggs, and like a modern-day Easter Egg Hunt, the eggs would be found in all sorts of hiding places wherever the hens had laid them, sometimes in the hay over the car.

While Leo was stationed as an airman at RCAF Summerside, he worked on aircraft electrical maintenance. After each airplane was repaired and ready for the air, I understand he became quite adept at convincing the pilots that it should be flight tested with him along to make sure everything was okay. I suspect the odd one of those flights may have required a long enough trip from Summerside to overfly the home place at Tatamagouche. Apparently there was a benefit to armed services personnel to have been overseas during the war, and Leo tried to argue that flying over the Northumberland Strait should be classed as being overseas.

My cousin Alec taught school for at least a year in the one room schoolhouse located in the district of Lake Road, to the east of Mattatal Lake. This would have been before Alec joined the air force. On one date in my mother's 1942 diary she mentions that Alec was back home because the Lake Road School was closed due to an outbreak of scarlet fever in the area. The school would have been in the general area of the Lake Road Methodist Church, which had been established there many years earlier.

Alec was an avid hunter and fisherman whenever he had time. He was always successful catching trout at the location of the old quarry site on the French River. I think he also used to fish for eels in the river during the winter. I remember a slim, ten-foot wooden pole with steel barbs on the end. A hole would have been chopped through the ice in a deep area of the river known to have a muddy bottom. Then the pole would have been manhandled through the hole until the barbs poked into the river bottom mud. Eels bury themselves in the mud in winter so it was a matter of poking in a different spot each time until an eel was speared. Sometimes a series of holes had to be cut in the ice to cover a wider area.

Katherine also became a school teacher and at one time in the early 1940s, taught elementary grades at the Tatamagouche School on Church Street. Some of her students that I would have known were: Loretta Coulter, Jean Langille, Joan Buckler, Ken MacDonald, and Lloyd Bryden.

My cousin Jane was almost the same age as my sister Laurel, being ten years older than me. Jane and my sister went to school together, walking back and forth the two miles each day to the school in the village. Living so near to us, Jane and my sister were very close friends (as well as first cousins). Jane often came to visit us after school and I remember a couple of times that she brought me a small end of blackboard chalk to play with.

Laurel and Jane would also have gone to school with Ron Joyce, who grew up in the village and eventually owned Tim Horton's before he sold it to Wendy's for four hundred million dollars. Ron Joyce was also brought up by a single mother, Grace Jollymore, and at that time would have been just as poor as the rest of us. Ron was a good friend of Junior Fulton who died of leukemia when he was ten years old.

Laurel and Jane both attended CGIT (Canadian Girls in Training), which met in the Community Hall with Mrs. Dan Murray (Anne Murray's grandmother) as leader. The girls studied programs such as home nursing, cooking and other domestic activities.

It was about the time that Jane graduated from high school that Aunt Kate and Jane moved from the house at the farm on the Lake Road to the MacLeod house in the village. This house was located on the Urquhart property directly across the street and up the hill from the present Fulton Pharmacy. Kate and Jane lived in this house until they moved to Truro.

When Jane graduated from high school, she took a six week teacher training course over the summer at the Normal College in Truro. She then obtained a teaching position for a year at the one room school on the Sand Point Road at Barrachois. On several occasions during the winter, she was known to walk across the ice of Tatamagouche Harbour from Steele's Island to reach the village. It was from her I learned about the Mi'kmaq burial ground on Steele's Island as she described seeing the stone marker with a cross etched on it. Jane later went on to receive her Doctorate in Education and became a professor at the Nova Scotia Teacher's College. She founded the Jane Norman College to train educational assistants for Early Childhood Education.

I was always closest to Jane of any of the first cousins on my father's side of the family. Jane taught me to swim, in the river behind the Norman home. Once, after a lot of hinting, she bought me a BB gun for my eleventh birthday, long before I was legally old enough to own one. Jane on a couple of occasions took me on exploration walks along the banks of the French River where she pointed out and described the various types of flora and fauna. We also dug clams on the sand bar opposite the Norman property.

There was the outline of an old settler's road that curved down the hillside to the north of the Norman house. This would have provided access to the marsh and the main river in earlier times. The ten-foot wide Wilson Creek at the foot of the hill was crossed by a causeway of field stones, dumped in the creek many years before. When I was first shown the crossing by my cousins, the surface appeared to have settled into the muddy creek bottom by several feet, the depth it was then below the level of the adjoining marsh on both sides. Maybe it has disappeared completely by now. My father or Aunt Kate claimed though that when they were younger the rock causeway was high enough that it would trap fish in the outgoing tide.

I had two other aunts on my father's side that also lived in the area. Aunt Fan and Uncle Fenton Weatherbie lived on Weatherbie's Point in Barrachois on the opposite side of Tatamagouche Harbour. They had five children: Harold, Don, Emma, Anne and Elmer. Tragically, Harold drowned at age eleven when he slipped away by himself and went swimming in the harbour. All were older than me, but Elmer was closest in age. We visited back and forth with Aunt Fan and Uncle Fenton occasionally, but less often due to the distance. Aunt Fan was the only one of my five aunts who had not gone to the USA before the Depression. The other four had all gone to Boston to train as nurses. Aunt Jane and Aunt Laura were the only two of my father's sisters to stay in the United States once they left Tatamagouche. I had first cousins in the Boston area and on the West coast with whom I have never had any contact.

Auntie Anne and Uncle Bill Ward were the family members my parents seemed to be closest to. Anne and Bill had come back from United States a bit earlier than my parents and they bought a house on Main Street, just across the street from Dr. Murray's home and office. Uncle Bill was a Stationary Engineer, so he had been able to get a very good full-time job tending the boiler and doing electrical and mechanical maintenance work at the Tatamagouche Creamery. It was Uncle Bill Ward who "Boiler Bob" at the present creamery interpretive centre would have been modelled after. They had one son, William Junior, who sometimes came to the farm to help with the haying. William served overseas in England and Holland with the Canadian Army near the end of the war.

William junior became a teacher and education administrator after he returned from overseas at the end of the war. He wrote several keys, or "Cole's Notes", to the Shakespeare plays we studied in high school English classes. William was married twice and had a daughter Elizabeth Anne, with his second wife, Elizabeth Garrett, of New Glasgow.

We used to go back and forth for dinners with Auntie Anne and Uncle Bill on the occasional Sunday and at Christmas and Easter. Auntie Anne made the best donuts, and if my father and I were on an errand to the village, we would usually drop in at Auntie Anne's for a treat. Anne and Bill had a shed out back of the house where my father could leave the horse if necessary. Smith MacPherson had his blacksmith shop further up the same lane so we would visit Auntie Anne at times when waiting for the horses to be shod.

We would also go on occasion to visit Alec Clark, a first cousin of my father, who lived further up the Lake Road, on the farm adjoining our woodlot. Alec's parents were Uncle Henry and Aunt Etta, my father's uncle and aunt. Uncle Henry would have been second generation of the Clarks who emigrated to Tatamagouche from Scotland. Alex was younger than my father, but they seemed to be very good friends and Alex would work together with my father in the woods on occasion. Alex had four children: Dawn, Marguerite, Gordon and Roger. Marguerite continues to live on the home place, first farmed by my great grandfather Charles.

I remember Uncle Henry telling me the story of how religious the Clark family had been when he was growing up. The early Clarks had been very devout Presbyterians. Uncle Henry had had a jackknife as a boy, but on Sunday the knife had to be put up on the kitchen shelf for the day so he would not be distracted by playing with it on the Sabbath.

We had lots of other relatives in the Tatamagouche area, by blood and by marriage. Most of them at that time were second or third cousins and there were many other connections by marriage because of the number of early immigrants who had come from the same areas of Scotland to settle in Tatamagouche. There would have been five or six families still with the Clark surname in and around Tatamagouche, all descendants of my great great-grandparents, John and Jane (Cooper) Clark.

My great great-grandparents with their family had come from Insch, Scotland, in the mid 1840s, and settled further up the Lake Road on property just outside the DesBarres Grant. The Clark Cemetery is located near the back of this property.

The Cooper family, on my great great-grandmother Jane's side had come out to Tatamagouche prior to the Clarks and had settled in the Cooper's Bridge area of the French River. Apparently, it was they who enticed the Clarks to come to Tatamagouche following the family's economic difficulties back in Scotland.

* * *

On September 1, 1951, my sister Laurel, and Russell Chester Swansburg, of Little Harbour, Shelburne County, were married at the farm. This was a momentous occasion that involved my parents in much planning, preparation, and effort to make the house and property spic and tidy. The ceremony was held in the living room of the house. I am not sure how the fifty guests would have fit inside, but obviously they would have spilled over into the den, hall and dining room.

My Uncle Bob Braine, who was minister at that time at St. John's United Church in Halifax, performed the marriage ceremony. My cousin Joan Braine played the piano for the wedding music. Mrs Anne Ward, aunt of the bride and Mrs Russell Kaiser, aunt of the groom presided over the tea service. Assisting in serving at the reception were Cousin Jane Norman and Ruth Forbes of Denmark and Mabel Murray of River John, nursing classmates of the bride. Mrs C.G. Fulton cut the ices, and Mrs J.P. White, Mrs F.R. Buckler, Mrs D.R. Bell, and Miss Anne Lombard replenished.

Previous to the wedding the bride was on the nursing staff of the Royal Jubilee Hospital in Victoria, BC, and the groom was a student at Western Reserve University in Cleveland, Ohio. They had met originally as nursing students, Laurel at the Victoria General in Halifax and Russ at the Nova Scotia Hospital in Dartmouth. Following their marriage, the couple resided in Cleveland while Russell completed his university degree.

A small anecdote I have since learned from my cousin Linda Braine concerned the state of mind of my sister in the hour prior to the wedding. While my sister was getting dressed and waiting with her mother in her bedroom upstairs, she began to have cold feet about the impending ceremony. Linda was called upstairs to help calm the nerves and lend encouragement for Laurel to make her way down the stairs to the waiting guests below.

* * *

My grandparents, Dr. Lawrence and Jessie Braine, lived in Annapolis Royal until the late 1940s when they moved to Glen Margaret, Halifax County, supposedly to semi-retire. My grandfather was a general practice doctor, and in those days doctors made house calls. My grandfather, while living in Annapolis, covered an extensive area radiating out from town to the Bay of Fundy shore, and outward in all directions until he reached areas covered by other doctors in Bridgetown or Digby.

These were in times before Medicare, when doctors had to collect their fees directly from their patients. Money was scarce in rural areas. Time and time again people would not have cash to pay for a doctor's visit. It was not uncommon for my grandfather to arrive back from a medical call with a bushel of apples or a haunch of deer meat or other articles of farm produce in lieu of his monetary fee.

I discovered in an old notebook of my grandfather's a copy of his scale of professional fees during the 1930s. Some of these procedures were as listed below:

- Each house visit within ½ mile of the office, from 7AM to 9PM - $1.00

- Night visit within ½ mile of the office, from 9PM to 7AM - $2.00 to $4.00

- Addition of Mileage beyond 1/2 mile of office - $0.50

- Office consultations - $1.00

- Venereal cases - $5.00

- Urinary analysis - $1.00

- Vaccinations - $1.00

- Ordinary maternity /midwifery cases - $8.00 to $15.00

- Complicated, instrumental or operative maternity cases - $12.00 to $25.00

- Reducing fractures or dislocations of large bones - $10.00

- Gynaecological examinations -$2.00

- Major operations - $10.00 to $100.00

- Minor operations - $1.00 to $10.00

- Administrating anaesthetics - $5.00 to $10.00

- Extracting teeth - $0.25 to $0.50

- Abortions and miscarriages - $8.00 to $15.00

- Post mortem examinations - $5.00

- Illness, accident or death certificates -$0.50

- Detention per day in medico legal cases - $10.00

My grandfather always had a car to make his house calls. During the war years, as a doctor, he was not subject to gasoline rationing. More often than not though in those early years, the dirt roads to neighboring communities would be virtually impassible to the automobile at times other than during the summer and fall seasons. For the adverse weather and road conditions he maintained a small barn at his residence, located across the street from what is now the Annapolis Royal Historical Gardens, and kept a horse or two to travel to outlying areas by buggy, sleigh, or on horseback. It was not an easy life during inclement weather and sometimes he would be storm-stayed at a patient's home if it was unsafe to travel any distance to get back home. Oftentimes he slept overnight in his office, which was located next to the telegraph office, just across St George Street from Fort Anne.

My mental picture of my grandfather Braine was of him always being professionally dressed as a doctor in those times. It was quite the sartorial image. He would have been dressed in a suit at all times with white shirt and tie and a vest hiding the suspenders under the suit coat. A gold chain would hang across the front of the vest attached to the gold pocket watch tucked in the left side pocket of his vest. His black shoes would be polished to a reflective shine and a pair of grey spats would be around his ankles. He wore gold wire-rimmed eyeglasses, and always sported a bushy mustache.

* * *

It might be useful to my family to at this point provide the bit that I know of our family medical history. My father suffered a debilitating stroke in his early eighties that left him in a wheelchair until he died at age 86. He had previously had and recovered from two mild heart attacks. My mother died at age 87 following several years of Alzheimer's Disease. Dementia was not so common when I was growing up and was then called "hardening of the arteries". My mother had had her gall bladder removed sometime during her middle age and I seem to remember her having a breast lump removed at about the same age. My sister had a stroke at age 60 which left her arm paralyzed and with limited mobility until she passed away at the age of 91. My grandfather on my mother's side died of a sudden heart attack on his way to a medical house call at the age of 77. He had been healthy and active in his medical practice up to the time that happened. My grandmother on my mother's side during all the time I remember her, was severely hunchbacked and bent out of shape with curvature of the spine. My grandfather on my father's side died at age 73 after a six-month illness reputed to be liver disease. My grandmother on my father's side was sickly and suffered from dementia for several years before she died in her early seventies. My aunt Laura Clark (Blechschmidt) died of "paralysis" from a stroke at age 52. Auntie Anne Ward and Aunt Kate Norman both had extremely high blood pressure in their later years. My first cousin Jane Norman died of ALS. I am not aware of any pertinent information on other close family members.

My uncle Bob Braine was severely colour blind. Since the colour blindness gene travels down through the female side, through my mother, there are some shades of red and green that I do not see normally. In that way my daughter's sons will also be prone to this affliction, and so on to their daughter's sons.

My father and my maternal grandfather both smoked tobacco most of their lives, as did virtually every man until the latter part of the 1900s, when the detrimental health effects of smoking finally became more widely recognized. My father mostly smoked a pipe except when he received cigarettes as a gift at Christmas or when relatives brought them from the United States when they came to visit. I remember back in the late 1940s that a carton of ten packages of Camel cigarettes cost $2.20. My father's pipe tobacco came in a pocket pouch or in a half pound tin. "Picobac" was his favorite brand. The Picobac tin was cylindrical, about five inches high and five in diameter. It cost 65 cents. When travelling by car with my father and my grandfather, they would both be smoking, and the air inside the car would be blue.

* * *

In coming to the end of this chapter I must implore the reader not to judge too harshly the actions, opinions and beliefs of our forebears. It was a much different society back then with different cultural norms from the way we experience our lives today. Beliefs we may cringe at as seeming so foreign to us today were the perpetuation of old attitudes passed down from generation to generation. We should simply be thankful that with the passage of time, the evolution of education and technology has meant that our generation is generally more enlightened in our attitudes nowadays.

CHAPTER 6 - SCHOOL

As mentioned in an earlier chapter, the old Tatamagouche School was located on the south side of Church Street opposite the present fire hall. Early pictures show the building as two stories, with one classroom per story, but without having the south annex. I understand that the annex to house Grade 1 and 2 was built in 1930 by Lawson Reid, a house builder from the Brule area. Lawson Reid also built several homes in the village, namely Jimmy MacKeen's on Main, Jim Menzie's on Pine, his own house on Pine, and Merle Hayman's on Maple.

In recent correspondence with Sybil Henderson Crawford, she referred me to a picture of herself and her schoolmates, including my sister Laurel and cousin Jane Norman, dated 1944. This picture is of students in the senior grades and included Judith Lockerby (Camozzi), Patty Brown, Hazel Cole (Miller), Dora Waugh (Reid), Jane Norman Grade 10, Grace Weatherby, Barbara Weatherby (Day), Dorothy Weatherby (Fraser), Isobel Ferguson (Ainslie), Sybil Henderson (Crawford) Grade 9, Laurel Clark (Swansburg) Grade 10,

Hazel Cunningham (MacKay), Sandy MacKay, Jim Ferguson, and Carol Wood (Tevlin).

I started school in Tatamagouche in the fall of 1945, when I was almost seven years old. The war was still being fought in Europe and the Far East. I started in Grade 1, with Miss Hilda Langille as my teacher, and I had Miss Langille in both Grade 1 and Grade 2. Tatamagouche had a three-room school at that time with Grades 1 and 2 in the single room south annex, Grades 3 to 8 in the one main floor room, and Grades 9 to 11 in the room on the top floor. Grade 12 was not taught in Tatamagouche. My sister, Laurel, who would have been in Grade 12 the year I started school, went off to Annapolis Royal to live with my grandparents and take her Senior Matriculation at the Annapolis Royal Academy. She and I never attended school together.

In a recent conversation with Hazel Cunningham, a schoolmate of Laurel's, she told me my sister missed a lot of time from school in Tatamagouche. Much of this I suspect was due to stormy weather and not choosing to walk the two miles back and forth to school. Hazel thought that my mother had home-schooled Laurel on these absences from class. I do know from my mother's 1942 diary that some of the missed days were due to my mother keeping Laurel home to babysit me while she went to one of her social events.

Attending school in the elementary grades was quite a different experience from how classrooms function today. Student's desks were bolted to the floor and were attached together in rows from the teacher's desk to the back of the classroom, all facing the teacher at her desk. The top of each desk had a hole in the upper right corner for an ink bottle and there was a shallow shelf under the desktop to store Hilroy scribblers, pencil boxes and crayons. Each desk formed part of the back of the seat in front, so if a girl was in the seat ahead her hair might hang over the desktop behind. Aisles went down the length of the room to separate the grades in the room. Anytime we were not working we were required to sit up straight in our seats with our hands folded on top of the desk.

A "strap" was prominently displayed on the top of the teacher's desk for the good behavior enforcement of miscreant students. The strap was a piece of quarter inch thick, rubberized industrial belting cut to be about two inches wide and a foot long. When punishment was deemed to be appropriate by a teacher the strap was applied vigorously to the open hands of the offending student.

One other thing worth mentioning in my Grade 1 and 2 classroom was a two foot high bomb of the type that was dropped out of airplanes during the war. This bomb was used as a doorstop in the entryway from the playground. I am certain that it was a dummy or had been defused, but it was realistic in every other way. During those times we thought of it only for its use to keep the door open, but can you imagine that sort of thing in a school today?

In those early grades we all belonged to Junior Red Cross. Each year, we would receive a pinback with a red cross on it we could wear on our caps. Pinbacks were a fad back then with some coming in cereal boxes such as Kellog's Pep, with the cereal brand or a newspaper cartoon character pictured. These pinbacks became popular trading items for kids who collected them.

Playing marbles indoors was a rainy-day recess activity. That evolved into rolling pennies against a wall and whoever was closest won the others. A stop was quickly put to that as it was deemed by our elders to be a form of gambling. The playground outside contained a single swing and a single plank teeter totter. There was also a small ball diamond where the older boys sometimes organized a pickup game of baseball. The girls' most common activity was skipping rope and playing hopscotch.

Lessons were taught by the teacher writing information and arithmetic exercises on the blackboards at the front and sides of the room, using white chalk. Our work was to copy everything from the blackboard into our Hilroy scribblers and to do the exercises. Often times, someone would be called to the board to answer an arithmetic question there. We had to memorize the multiplication tables up to twelve times twelve and learn to do multiplication and long division on paper or on the blackboard.

Included in our studies in those times was learning the English Imperial System of weights and measures. Of all the useful creations of significance by the British throughout history, I cannot comprehend how this completely illogical system managed to exist as long as it did.

Besides yards, feet, and inches broken down into halves, quarters, eights, sixteenths, and thirty-seconds, we learned that distances were measured in rods, chains, furlongs and miles. Area was measured in square feet and acres, an acre being 43,560 square feet and there were 640 acres in a square mile. Weights were measured in drams, ounces, pounds and tons. Farm produce was measured in pecks and bushels. To further complicate things, distances on water were measured in nautical miles, fathoms and leagues. For cooking there were teaspoons and tablespoons, cups and fractions thereof, pints, quarts and gallons. The American gallon was different than the Imperial gallon, and there was a difference between regular and Troy ounces.

In one corner of the Grades 1 & 2 classroom was a sand table. One of the projects with the sand table was to create what was supposed to be a native village complete with miniature birch bark canoes and wigwams.

The school was heated by a coal fired furnace in the basement and the Grade 1 and 2 section of the building had one large open-grated hot-air register in the centre of the classroom floor. I remember Miss Langille standing over this register to warm herself while teaching our classes, with the warm rising air rippling the fabric of her skirt.

My other teachers in the elementary grades were: Miss Rowena Bushie, in Grade 3, Mrs. Melita Weatherbie (later Alec Clark's wife) in Grade 4, and Miss Harriett Gourley in Grade 5.

Our farm was actually situated in the French River school district and I should have attended the one-room school further up the Lake Road. Jimmy and Curtis MacKinnon, who lived closer to Tatamagouche, went to the school in French River. We used to meet each other walking in opposite directions to school.

Some of the kids I started school with were Clayton Langille, Morris Cole, Lawrence Weatherbie, Ron Campbell, David Menzie, David MacKeen, Dave Cock, Helen Cunningham, Evelyn Coulter, Vesta MacBurnie, Sandy Byers, Annette MacLeod, Leona Mattatall, Tillie Tucker, Ida Brown and Janice Jardine. There were others whose names escape me now or who only lived in Tatamagouche for a short time. I think the school Principal at that time was Miss Isobel Creaser, who soon became Mrs. Willis Bonnyman.

With my sister gone to Annapolis Royal for her Grade 12, I would have had to travel back and forth to school by myself. I don't think I attended school much that first year, even though I would have been seven years old just one month after I started. I think my mother decided she was going to home school me most of that year. She had taught in a little one room school at West Dalhousie (Annapolis County) during her first year out of high school, and she considered herself a teacher. The other thing that happened either during my first or second year was that I spent most of the winter home sick with "swollen glands," or what is now known as mononucleosis. Nevertheless, from the start of school until Grade 7, I always had the highest marks in exams and ended up with the prize for the highest average in my grade at the end of each school year.

School closures due to stormy weather did not happen very often. Snow days for me were only when the Lake Road was blocked for a day or more at a time. At the time, the Lake Road was a narrow gravel road that tended to drift over badly in a blizzard. The section east of the Wilson Creek Bridge to Davy Bell's house was especially bad because the road was quite a bit lower than the surrounding fields and it filled in with snow drifts with a minimal amount of wind. The government snow clearing equipment was limited to a road grader with a plow on front, or a bulldozer, so we often had to wait a long time for the road to be opened. I have a picture of the road grader plow trying to push its way through snow up to the height of its cab windows. Davy Bell had a three-ton truck with a plow, and if the snow was not too deep he would sometimes clear the road up as far as our lane.

Back in those times the government used to install "snow fences" in areas subject to extreme drifting. These fences were made of wooden slats interwoven with fence wire to hold the slats in place. They would be attached to a line of fence posts one hundred feet into an open field from the roadway. The theory was that blowing snow would accumulate in the lee of the fence and there would be less of it to fill in the roadway itself. The practise of snow fencing died out with the transition to all weather roads.

I learned to read early and easily. My mother had a copy of one of the old Grade 1 readers and I can still visualize the beginning lesson: "Here I am, my name is Nan." From that early beginning under the tutelage of my mother I read voraciously. I never did any sports in school except during Phys Ed classes in high school, where I learned to play badminton and volleyball. I choose instead to read at every opportunity available. I started by going through all the Thornton W. Burgess animal books, and then moved on to the Hardy Boys and all of my sister's teenage books. In the days before there was a library in Tatamagouche, the Provincial bookmobile used to come to the school every couple of weeks, and I would borrow the maximum number of books that I was allowed each trip. I credit a large part of my formal education to all the books I read over the years.

We spent many hours practicing to improve our cursive handwriting during grade three. We had a lined workbook to help us, perhaps the MacLean method. By following the examples given, we had to do pages of circles, ovals and straight lines, all within the printed lines of the workbook pages. Any spare time we had, other than when the teacher was giving a lesson or when we worked on exercises in our scribblers, we had to take out our workbook and practice our cursive writing. Anyone trying to read my writing nowadays would probably suggest I should have spent more time practicing.

During those middle elementary grades, we also had class spelling bees. At the appointed time each day, the class would be lined up along one wall of the classroom. The teacher would start at the head of the line and ask each student in order to spell one word from the list of words we had to learn for that particular day. If the student misspelled the word then he or she had to go to the end of the line. The challenge was always to get to the head of the line and stay there for succeeding days. I usually managed to stay in that position unless

I missed a day of school, which meant I had to start from the back end of the line again.

It seemed that once or twice in January or February each winter there would be a major rainstorm and thaw, and when the temperature turned cold again there would be huge patches of ice in the field at the front of the farm. This was where I learned to skate. One year I was able to rig up a sail on a sled so that in a good wind I could travel several hundred feet at a time across the icy field. I also had an old toboggan, and would go by myself after school to coast on the hillside back of the farm and down onto the marsh. The hillside was all open cow pasture at that time with very few trees, so it was a great place to coast.

At some time during my early school years there was an outdoor rink, with boarded sides all around, built at the lower side of the community field. This was directly across the street from where the RCMP detachment is now located. I do not think it lasted very long. Its use would have been unpredictable, subject to weather conditions and dependent on the formation of natural ice.

When the old Tatamagouche elementary school closed, replaced by the more modern, one story elementary school on the same site, the south annex was disconnected and I understand it was moved through the village and relocated behind the Ernie MacDonald residence, just up the hill from the train station. It is now a part time antique shop owned by Lawrence Cole. Tommy Pugh may have moved the remainder of the old school building over onto his property next door, but I am not sure of that.

* * *

I received my first watch when I was in about Grade 3. It was a Westclox Dax pocket watch with a polished steel case, had a white face with blue centre, and cost between two and three dollars from the Eaton's catalogue. It had to be wound once a day. But it was rugged and it survived all the activities I was involved in for several years. When I was in Grade Six, I was given a new wrist watch as a reward for my good marks in my year end exams. It too came from Eaton's and was called a nurse's watch. In my mind, the neat thing about that watch was that the hands glowed in the dark, which meant that I could tell the time at night without turning on a light. That watch also survived a lot of abuse and I still have it in my possession.

Something else I have carried in my pocket going back as far as elementary school days is a jackknife. I certainly lost a number of them over the years, but I have always considered a jackknife as an accessory that I want to have in my pocket. One use for a jackknife back when I was a boy was to make a wooden whistle out of a short stick of green alder or willow.

My other priority has always been to have some cash with me at all times. This goes back to my early years when money was so scarce, making me feel a need to always have some cash in my wallet in case of an emergency. One time, when I was not very old, I was given a dime, which I squirreled away. When my mother eventually found it, I was given the dickens for hiding it because any money at that particular time was needed for essentials.

* * *

During almost all my years of school I brought a lunch from home. I lived the farthest distance from school of anyone in my grade, so most times in elementary school I ate alone in my classroom at noon when the other kids would all have gone home for lunch. Sometimes the teacher would be there, sometimes not.

In late elementary, I had a rectangular metal Roy Rogers lunch box with a carry handle. Lunch would have consisted of a homemade bread sandwich and cookies or a piece of cake, and a glass bottle of milk. Sandwiches were of roast beef, chicken, ham, egg, or chokecherry jelly. My favorite was a fried egg sandwich. Sometimes there would be mashed potato and bacon or sausage, and during lobster season in spring there would be lobster sandwiches. Sometimes, instead of a sandwich, there would be a hardboiled egg still in the shell with a bit of salt and pepper wrapped in wax paper to go with it.

I believe it would have been sometime about 1950, that Howard LeFresne and his wife, Jimmy's parents, established the Sunrise Bakery on Main Street. Following the 1953 village fire, the bakery was relocated to a new building on the site of the Lester Buckler store that had been destroyed in the fire. With the new bakery in town it was now possible to actually buy fresh bakery bread and use that bread in sandwiches for lunches at school.

For a year or so in elementary school I went to Mrs. Frances White's house for lunch. She was a member of my mother's bridge club, and some of the teacher's boarded with her. I think my mother supplied her with eggs and cream in payment for my lunches. What I remember most was that we always had fish on Friday. Rice pudding with raisins in it was a popular dessert.

Frances and Jimmy White lived in the house that is now a Chinese Restaurant across the street from Sharon Church. Their children were Shirley and Terry, who bracketed me in age. On the east side of the Whites was the home of Harold Menzie and his wife, whose son David was my age. The house to the west of Whites belonged to Bruce Tucker and his wife, Floyd's parents. The next house beyond Tuckers was Wes MacLennan and his wife, Anne's parents.

There were other kids close by in that Church Street/Main Street area. Thus it was with my lunch connection to the Whites that I was included in an early birthday party celebration for Terry White. This had to have been the first kids' birthday party that I had ever been invited to. What made this especially memorable was that the birthday cake had tiny prizes wrapped in waxed paper buried in the cake. The cake was carefully cut so that each child's piece of cake included one of the little wrapped gifts, which were nickel coins, pinbacks, or other tiny articles which we could all consider as treasures.

I never cared much for school and counted the days until the end of the school year in June. My best year was Grade 6, when I had Miss Florence Mowatt for teacher. Miss Mowatt was young, pretty, and just out of Normal College. Once, on a sunny Saturday in early spring she took all the boys in the class on a fishing trip up to Donaldson's Bridge on the French River.

* * *

I switched to the Tatamagouche Rural High School when I started Grade VII. This would have been the second year after the school opened. Suddenly I was amongst about 350 other students from Grade VII to Grade XII. All but the village kids travelled by school bus. The area covered was from River John/Welsford to Wallace, and from Wentworth to Earltown. I was entitled to ride the bus, but I only ever did if there was a storm or if I did not have an alternate ride. My bus route went from the school to Bayhead, then across to Lake Road almost up to Mattatall Lake, and then back to the school. I was on the last end of the circuit so it was quicker for me to walk home after school than take the bus for half an hour.

My homeroom teacher when I started in Grade VII at TRHS was Miss Sylvia Langille. There were enough students for two classes of Grade Sevens; 7A and 7B. I was in Grade 7A. Some of the other kids in that first class would have been Ron Campbell, Peter Jollymore, Ron Hickey, Sandy Byers, Dorothy Trenholm, Jimmy Craig, John Ross, Joan Reid, Phyllis Drysdale, Helen Cunningham, Vaughan Langille, Bob Chapman, Joan Spence, Helen Elliott, Eldon

Forbes, Audrey Winmill, Ken Halverson, Don Hayman, Marjorie MacNab, Josephine Awalt, Bill MacKay and others whose names elude me now.

 Back in those times if I was walking to or from school, someone would usually stop and offer me a drive. It did not matter if we did not know who it was back then. I remember once catching a ride with a couple from the States, who were visiting relatives further up the Lake Road. They were driving a Model A Ford Coupe and I rode in the rumble seat of the Coupe. A rumble seat was a seat for two people located in trunk area of the car. The trunk cover opened backwards and formed the back of the seat. Thus the passengers were exposed to open air behind the cab of the car.

Whenever I walked the two miles home from school I walked alone as there was no one else my age that travelled in the same direction. Laurie Tattrie lived across from where the bowling alley is now and had an unfriendly dog that ran loose. I usually took a detour through Duncan Marshall's hay field to avoid having to walk past the dog.

* * *

In the spring of 1952, there was a devastating polio epidemic that affected wide areas of the country. One of my fellow high school students was Harold Pugh, who was a couple of years older than me. He contracted the disease and was taken to Halifax and placed in an iron lung. There was a general fear of how contagious this disease was, so the powers-that-be closed the schools for a period of time. I know we were out of school for a number of weeks because the teachers mailed out packages of homework and assignments to work on at home, so we would not fall too far behind in our curriculum. I remember one of my science projects was to take a grain of corn, fold it in a damp cloth to germinate, and then to record its growth each day.

There were others at the school who contracted polio at that time, including (I believe) the principal, Gordon Hayes, and at least one female student. Harold spent nearly a year in the Polio Clinic before he passed away. The 1953 TRHS yearbook was dedicated to the memory of Harold by his fellow students.

Polio, or poliomyelitis, was an infectious disease that had been more commonly known in earlier years as infantile paralysis. In one of my mother's August 1942 diary entries she mentioned that the Sunday church service on that particular day had not been held due to a case of infantile paralysis in the community.

There was one other medical scare that occurred, though I am not sure of the year. One of the girls in my grade contracted scarlet fever. In those times that disease was considered very contagious, and serious, so that the girl's whole family was quarantined in their own home for an extended period of time. I remember seeing the large notice posted on the family's front door warning people not to enter the home.

* * *

When I was in high school, the school day began at 9AM with a short period of devotions. The classes in every grade took a turn, one week at a time, to prepare for and present the short devotional program. This was usually comprised of an opening prayer, a Scripture reading and the singing of a hymn. Each day of the week that a class was responsible for the devotion, the class members involved would all crowd into the Principal's office to be able to speak into the PA system, so it could be broadcast to every room in the school. One particular hymn I remember our Grade XII class learning and singing was "Will Your Anchor Hold in the Storms of Life." It was all a very Protestant style service.

One other thing that was instilled in us during high school was that we would always stand at rigid attention for the National Anthem, with heads uncovered, eyes forward, and arms straight at our sides with hands fisted and thumbs pointed down and touching our pant legs. I cringe nowadays when young people do not know enough to take off their caps or to even stand still for O Canada.

Several of my male teachers in high school were veterans who had gone into teaching once the war was over. My geography teacher was Fred Campbell, who was originally from the Brookfield area. Mr. Campbell had been in the RCAF during the war. Whenever the opportunity presented itself in class, someone would ask Mr. Campbell some question that would lead into his war experiences. The objective was to get him to tell us some long anecdote. We were usually quite successful in getting him to use up most of the geography period that way.

Mr. Wylie Dill was my geometry teacher and he was also ex-RCAF. He was the commanding officer of our high school Air Cadet squadron. Mr. Dill's main focus at TRHS was on air cadet activities with the teaching of geometry less of a priority. When final exam time rolled around, the Geometry exam questions required the proving of a number of geometric theorems. Not well prepared, I simply wrote out the theorem itself on my foolscap sheet and passed it in, mostly blank. When the marks came out, I had a pass. I suspect that this was only because I had done well in the Air Cadet program.

Some of the other teachers I had in high school were: Sylvia Ross, English (she was Sylvia Langille when I had her in Grade 7); Violet Mattatall, Algebra (she must have been at least in her mid seventies at the time); Rufus Reid, Chemistry; Joyce Wright, Music (who once told my father I had a lovely bass voice); MacCara Cameron, Industrial Arts; Stuart Burbine, Phys Ed (he ended up after we had graduated, marrying Charlette Hartling, a girl in my class); J.W. Cameron, Biology (he had copies of all the Provincial final exam papers for the past twenty years or so and that is what he taught us); Eleanor Dimock, English Grammar; Betty Noiles, French (young pretty redhead who did not speak any French); and, Gordon Hayes, History and TRHS Principal. Mr. Hayes was an ex Army Captain and one of the best teachers I ever had.

Several other teachers in the high school over the years while I was there were: Marg Swan, who later became a Principal of the Nova Scotia Teachers' College; Don Cameron, who moved on to Mount Allison as a professor; Allie Flemming, who may also have taught at

Mt. A; and, Robert Danson, who became a professor at Teachers College.

Included in the school curriculum back in those times was a half day each week of Industrial Arts for the boys and a half day of Home Economics for the girls. These courses were a very good introduction to useful life skills which have proven beneficial in many of my activities over the years. Besides using carpentry tools on small woodworking projects such as turning out a Maple fruit bowl on the wood lathe, designing and making a hardwood gun rack, making a pine candle holder, making and tempering a metal screwdriver, etc. we learned drafting, metal working and basic mechanics. It is a shame that students nowadays no longer have access to a well-equipped shop to learn how to use basic handyman tools.

Back in those years the curriculum was set so that everyone in each individual grade took the same courses and followed the same class schedule. There were no optional courses. In one junior high grade we all studied Latin. By studying Latin, I gained a greater understanding of English and French grammar. I studied French all through high school, where we were taught to read and write in that language. However, the French teachers did not speak a single word of French. Although we learned the vocabulary and the grammar, we left school unable to speak or understand any oral French.

The Tatamagouche Rural High School colours were maroon and gold. The school crest had a stylized TRHS in maroon letters centered on a gold background, with the words "Finis Coronat Opus" in a banner above the TRHS, and a crossed badminton racket and baseball bat below. It was possible to buy a school jacket with Tatamagouche Rural High in gold letters across the back and the school crest in felt sewn on the front. Also available was a sterling silver school ring having the school crest. The cost of the ring was five dollars.

Elvis Presley rose to fame as a popular singer while I was in high school. One of my classmates, Vaughn Langille, did an exceptionally good imitation of Elvis. Vaughn sang and played guitar naturally, so with a turned-up collar and a duck tail haircut he was able to play the character of Elvis, long before the bevy of current impersonators. Vaughn became a popular performer at school and community variety concerts, ending up with his own fan club of teenage girls who clapped and screamed at all Vaughn's performances of Elvis songs.

Duck tail haircuts for the boys were a fad back in those days. Boys were able to shape their hair with Brylcreem. Brylcreem was a greasy hair styling product for men, which came packaged in a tube similar to toothpaste. All the boys used it to rub into their hair to slick it down into whatever shape they wished. It did not matter that this was probably the main contributor to dandruff. The hair cream was advertised on radio with a neat jingle starting with, "A little dab will do you, and the girls will pursue you."

The girls all wore dresses or skirts to school back then. The hems of dresses would all be well below the knee. Poodle skirts were a fashion item.

It was years before "Reach for the Top" would become a widely recognized competition in the high schools, but once when I was in Grade 8, a similar type of competition was held during an Assembly period. Two teams of five were picked from all the students in the school. I was chosen to be a member of one team though I do not have any idea why I would have been chosen. I remember that two other members of the team were Campbell Gunn and Ira Drysdale. One of my questions was to name the chemical essential in photosynthesis, for which I was able to answer chlorophyll. The other team won by one point that day, but it was a fun competition.

As I think back, I do not believe there were many discipline problems in high school, and I do not remember there being any serious bullying. In the junior high grades we were so regimented that there was very little opportunity for individual expressions of independence, hostile or otherwise. Because of bussing and the distances involved, there was little opportunity for organized sports or other after-school activities.

* * *

When I was in Grade 11 or 12, our Air Cadet Squadron hosted an Air Cadet Ball, in the high school auditorium. This Ball, which was opened up to members of the public who purchased tickets, was touted as a major social event for the village. The dress was semiformal with the Air Cadets and officers in our dress uniforms. The auditorium was decorated with colourful streamers strung from ceiling to walls, and the lighting was adjusted to present an elegant atmosphere. The Don Warner Orchestra, a well-known big band from Halifax, was engaged to come all the way from the city to provide the dance music. The shocker was that the ticket price was set at six dollars per couple by the squadron commanding officer. This ticket cost caused a lot of tongues to wag in the community since the price of admission to local dance halls was still in the fifty-cent range. Nevertheless, the Ball was well attended; everyone deemed it to be the fashion event of the year, and enough money was made to pay the orchestra.

Mrs. Frank Buckler, Joan's mother Clara, was a very good friend of my mother, and Clara had some connection to Florence MacKenzie, a girl in my grade from Malagash. Between Clara and my mother, I was set up to take Florence to the Ball. Clara did all the arranging. Florence wore a light yellow, long gown of some kind of wispy material. Clara provided a corsage of yellow roses, and put Florence up overnight so that I did not have to travel to Malagash. It was an enjoyable evening, but probably because at that age I considered the arrangement not of my own making, we did not pursue the alliance beyond that one evening.

* * *

At the end of Grade 12 we wrote two sets of final examinations. One was a set of school exams, prepared and corrected by the teacher of each subject, and the second set was supplied by the provincial Department of Education to every student in the Province. The school exams in Grade 12 counted for graduation activities, but the Provincial exams were used to determine if we received our Senior Matriculation. Provincial exam marks were necessary for continuing on to University or to other educational pursuits.

The high school prom and graduation were considered to be prestigious events. The prom was very formal, with the girls in colourful long gowns and the boys in suits and ties. The school auditorium was decorated with lots of crepe paper streamers. A live dance band would have been hired to play foxtrots and waltzes. Very few students were paired up or "going steady" at that time, so much deliberation was required in advance to decide who to invite to the prom. It was the boy's responsibility to do the inviting, and it took time to build up the initiative to approach a girl he might have his eye on to invite her to the dance. I invited Audrey Winmill, who was in my class, and she said yes. Audrey lived in River John, so I had to borrow my grandmother's car to use that evening.

Graduation too was stiff and formal. We did not have caps and gowns, so everyone had to be dressed in their very best attire. We marched into the auditorium in pairs to the music teacher playing "Pomp and Circumstance" on the piano. Instead of a valedictorian, the local bank manager had been invited as guest speaker. The man was well educated, but obviously was not a stand-up public speaker.

This turned out to be almost three quarters of an hour of the most tedious speech in my memory.

CHAPTER 7 - THE VILLAGE

Tatamagouche has a long and varied history. Unfortunately, many of the events of historical significance are little known except to those people who have a keen interest in historical matters and who are willing to dig for the information. I feel it is such a shame that we did not learn any of our local history when I was attending school. I am convinced it would have been much more interesting and more relevant in our future lives than memorizing the dates of sixteenth and seventeenth century wars in Europe. I have yet to discover any need for me to use the details of the rise and fall of the Holy Roman Empire in Europe

Before the coming of Europeans to the shores of Nova Scotia, Tatamagouche for centuries had been an important location for the indigenous Mi'kmaq peoples. The name Tatamagouche is derived from the native word which meant that the harbour entrance was restricted by a sandbar. Tatamagouche would have been a vital living area for these native people due to the easy access to salmon, trout, smelts and gaspereau in the two rivers; for oysters, clams and mussels along the shorelines; and for plentiful waterfowl and game in the harbour and forests. It was also located on a major travel route, the course of the French River being part of the transportation link between the Bay of Fundy and the Northumberland Strait.

The Acadians arrived about 1710 to establish a settlement at the mouth of the French River. Over the next four and a half decades, these French immigrants settled and farmed the marshes of the rivers, cleared upland, and established a vital trading port in the supply line from the Acadian settlements of the Annapolis Valley to the Fortress of Louisburg. Remnants of the Acadian dikes along the French River are still visible.

During these times, including the Acadian settlement at Tatamagouche, it seemed there were ongoing hostilities between the British and French along the eastern seacoast of what would later become Canada. An historic site monument located beside the new Tatamagouche library recognizes a significant naval battle that occurred just outside Tatamagouche Harbour. It is said that the outcome of this battle was a contributing factor in the capture of Louisburg by the British side.

Louisburg, on the eastern tip of Cape Breton, was a major military fortress for France to guard the entrance to North America. Much of the fresh food supply for Louisburg came from the Acadian settlements between Grand Pre and Port Royal. The trade route was by boat up the Bay of Fundy shore to Isgonish/Masstown, across the Cobequid hills to Tatamagouche, and thence by boat to Louisburg. This route was necessary because the British Navy controlled the Atlantic coastline of the colony.

An historical fact not widely known is that due to the importance of this supply link, Tatamagouche was the first settlement in Acadia to suffer the consequences of Governor Lawrence's decision in Halifax to expel all the Acadians from Nova Scotia. Much has been publicised about the Expulsion of the Acadians from Grand Pre, but this terrible act of forced removal of the Acadian people actually began at Tatamagouche.

On orders from the Governor, a unit of New England Militia under Captain Willard was dispatched from Fort Cumberland at Amherst, to march to Tatamagouche in early August of 1755. On his arrival, Captain Willard and his troops took all the Acadian men in the area as prisoners. He then ordered his soldiers to destroy by fire every dwelling, barn and storehouse in the settlement. Once this was accomplished, the male prisoners were marched off to Fort Cumberland where they were eventually loaded on British ships and sent down the Atlantic seacoast to the Carolinas. The Acadian women and children were cruelly abandoned by Willard at Tatamagouche, to fend for themselves in destitute circumstances.

(For more information on these historical events one should see Norris Whiston's research in his publication "Cobequid Meguma and Acadian Villages".)

* * *

Tatamagouche had two devastating fires while I was growing up. The first in about 1950 wiped out the central part of the north side of Main Street. The fire happened during the night and we received word at the farm by telephone that the village was on fire. We dressed and went quickly to the village where my father would have helped with the firefighting efforts. I remember standing somewhere on the hillside to the east of where Roy Kennedy's shop was located, in order to watch the roaring inferno across the street.

Fire fighting efforts to stop the spread of the fire were futile due to the lack of adequate equipment and the big old wooden buildings having been built too close together. I think that perhaps four or five prominent stores were completely destroyed that night. The loss of these stores dealt a devastating blow to the commercial life of the community. Another major fire occurred in 1953 on the same side of the street.

Before the fires there were a number of large stores located in that central section of Main Street. The Bank of Nova Scotia building was situated on the northeast corner of Main Street and Queen Street, the lane leading down to the Lynwood Inn operated by Miss Margaret (Mag) Patterson. The Bank Manager had living quarters in the back and upper floor of the bank building.

Next to the bank on the east side was a small shoe shop owned by George Clark. George also carried school supplies, which I remember may have been the greater part of his business. This George was the third generation George of that branch of the Clark family, and a second cousin of my father. Harry Annis also operated a shoe repair business out of this building.

Next to George was the Selrite Five and Ten store owned by James (Jimmy) White. On the east side of this store there was a walkway to gain entrance to the telephone office which occupied a back section of the Selrite building. Greta Bonnyman was one of the operators of the switchboard. I have an image in my mind of a visit to this office and seeing "Central" sitting in front to the switchboard with her large earphones wrapped over her head, plugging cords into the portholes in the vertical switchboard panel to switch various calls from phone line to phone line. The upper floor of the Selrite building was used by one of the Lodges; the IOOF or Eastern Star perhaps?

To the east of the Selrite building was a small shop which was Will MacQueen's meat market. Later on, when Will was less active in the meat business, he had a horse and buggy with which he happily gave rides to kids around the village. The horse could do tricks, one of which was to count out its age by tapping its front hoof on the ground for the number years of its age.

Next there was a right-of-way, a lane which led to the houses on the ridge that ran along the harbour shoreline in that back street area. This right-of-way was the break where the fire was stopped at its western end.

Next along the Main Street from that lane was the grocery store of Menzie and Langille. Harold Menzie operated the store. His son

David was in my grade during elementary school days. Jim Langille was the other part of the store partnership.

The next building was a hardware store operated by Reg Matheson and Ralph Bell, Warren Bell's son. I believe Hayman Brothers Hardware occupied that same location, but perhaps that was after the fire and before Henry and Harry Hayman built a new store west of Lloyd Campbell's BA service station. Merle Hayman operated the new store and I used to buy my fishing line, hooks and lead sinkers there. I would have also bought BBs there for my air rifle.

In one street level side of the Quality hardware building was located the C.G Fulton Nyal Drug store and ice cream parlor. Cecil Fulton operated out of three different buildings in my memory, the first two of which were ruined by fires. A cone of ice cream cost five cents at the soda counter in the drug store. For special customers (my mother's BFF was Jenny Fulton, Cecil's wife) the soda fountain would pack and sell a carton of the same, better quality ice cream that was used for cones. Back then the ice cream choices were limited to vanilla, chocolate, or strawberry, and possibly grape-nut. There was also a Simpson's order office at the Fulton pharmacy location.

Next was the Bonnyman and Bell general store, which sold groceries, meat and various items of general goods from clothing to hardware. This store had originally been built and operated by John Clark, Hallie Clark's grandfather. Davy Bell also operated Bell's Transfer, whose trucks brought freight from Truro and New

Glasgow. Harry Bonnyman also started a funeral home beside his house on Pine Street.

Next there was another lane leading to the houses behind. It is now called Riverside Drive, which loops around and comes back to join Main Street further east. On the east side of this right-of-way was a large grocery store owned and operated by Lester Buckler. This was a three-story building.

The next building east of the Lester Buckler store was a smaller building holding Baxter Fraser's tailor shop. Mr. Fraser was commonly known as Bax, which was pronounced as "Back". Fraser lived in the so-called Dr. Sedgwick house at the corner Church Street and Maple Avenue.

My memory does not serve me well on the next two stores, which were destroyed in the 1953 fire. I think the smaller of the two was owned by George Langille, who as I remember lived on the north side of Blair Avenue, next to the community field. I remember him as an old man sitting on his veranda when I would be walking home from elementary school.

East of the Langille building was a larger store that may have been a millinery store at one stage, but I believe David Van Tassel had his barber shop there at the time of the fire. Anyway, David's shop was destroyed in the fire and when he was able to get back up and running again in the same area, my father gave him a large mirror for the shop. This ornately framed mirror had come down to us from one of my relatives on my mother's side of the family and I'm guessing it was four feet by four feet in size, ideal for the opposite wall of the barber shop.

Next I believe there was a narrow open space before coming to Bill Langille's meat market. This building was at the east end of the 1953 fire, but it was substantially damaged and required extensive repairs before being able to open up again. Later in the 1950s, when I worked the summer at the new Bonnyman and Bell store, Lawrence Cole worked at Bill Langille's market. I remember Lawrence was paid twenty dollars a week and I felt lucky to be paid twenty-four dollars a week for virtually the same number of hours and the same type of work.

Beyond the meat market was Gordon MacBurnie's barber shop in the years before the 1950s. This was where I would have gotten my hair cut when I was a child. Gordon claimed that he used to come in to work in the shop at four in the morning for the benefit of men on their way to work who wanted an early shave. Haircuts were fifteen cents for youth and twenty-five cents for men.

Somewhere in the section just beyond the MacBurnie barber shop, Hans Coulter operated a jewellery store with a watch and clock repair business. This was before Hans started driving one of the school busses when the high school opened in 1951. I have a vague recollection that Dr. MacLeod, Annette's father, may have had a dentistry office in that general area for short period of time. Also in that general area, Isobel Byers operated a hat and dress shop in the early 1940s.

All of the stores between the Langille meat market and the MacQueen meat market were destroyed by the fires of 1950 and 1953. One earlier fire of memory happened December 26, 1946, which gutted a large section of the Sellrite store. My mother and I were actually shown the interior of the store shortly afterward by Frances White. I still have an image of the counters of inventory black with soot and of carefully walking around a hole in the aisle floor where the fire had burned its way through from below. This store, however, was able to be renovated without any major structural change.

On the opposite side of the street across from Bill Langille's meat market was the village band shell and behind it, further up the hill, was the Tatamagouche Inn. The Inn, built in 1832 as the Stirling Hotel, was operated by Harold and Grace Cassidy in the 1940s and by Frances Moss in the 1950s. In the 1948 Nova Scotia government publication "Where to Stay in Nova Scotia,", which gave accommodations information for Tatamagouche, the Tatamagouche Inn was listed as having 22 guest rooms and four bathrooms. The rooms were $2 and $3 per night. Breakfast was 75 cents, dinner $1 and supper 75 cents. It was advertised that there was salt water bathing, and trout fishing and hunting guides were available.

Just to the west of the hotel building was the residence of the hotel owner. Patsy Moss, who was a high school classmate of mine, lived in that house with her parents. To the west of that house were the Urquhart house and another residence on the hillside, set back some distance from the street. But out front and just to the west of the hotel entrance driveway in the 1950s was the post office, which was a former army building relocated from Debert. Westerly between that building and the New Annan Road was located the Ronald Perrin machine shop and Roy Kennedy's electrical shop. A huge siren was attached to the roof of Roy's shop, which was the fire alarm that was used to call for help whenever there was a fire. The siren was also sounded at twelve o'clock as a time signal to indicate the beginning of noon hour. The siren was loud enough that it could easily be heard at our farm two miles away.

Roy Kennedy was a multi talented guy. Besides being an electrician, he was the village fire chief, the regional game warden, and an expert on the history of the village. My mother's diary mentions having ordered a pressure cooker from Roy's shop, but once it arrived she was reluctant to use it, being afraid that it might blow up if the steam pressure was too great. For more information on local history please refer to Roy's publication, "Each in Turn."

I remember Roy more in his role as game warden. At one time in those years there was an overabundance of porcupines wreaking havoc on the woodland evergreen trees. In an attempt to control the porcupine population, the government instituted a fifty cent bounty on the animals. But in order to collect the bounty one had to cut off the porcupine's snout and take it to Roy for verification. Roy had to be astute in his inspection as some unscrupulous person might also cut the footpads of the animal, punch two eyeholes in them and try to pass then off as snouts.

Diagonally across the intersection of Main Street and Maple Avenue, and directly in front of the present Canadian Legion building, was a small building housing the law office of William Nelson. Billy Nelson, as he was referred to by most villagers, was an active member of Sharon United Church. He volunteered as a Sunday School teacher and Clerk of Session, and was also a long time Scout leader. In his early years he acted for a time as Principal of the Tatamagouche School. Throughout his life he had an interest in local history and collected many historical records. My image of him is an older gentleman seen through the front window of his office, sitting at his desk surrounded by his law books. Nelson Park was created and named in his memory.

* * *

Other members of the Clark family were prominent residents of the area in the century following their immigration from Scotland. The head of the family on arrival, my great great grandparents John and Jane Clark, settled on the Lake Road at Millbrook, on land still occupied by their heirs. The Clark cemetery is located on that property. John had been a slate quarryman back in Scotland when that occupation fell on hard times. Jane was uneducated, having signed her name with an "X" on legal documents. There are many letters copied in the "Clark" book, written by John before and after leaving Scotland, to keep in touch with relatives on both sides of the Atlantic.

The Clark sons and daughters who came to Tatamagouche with their parents were:

1) Robert, who also settled on the Lake Road near his parents, had ten children, most of whom migrated to the western United States. Robert had a hard life, suffering with prostate cancer at the end, and he drowned himself in the brook at the back of the farm.

2) James left Tatamagouche for four years to partake in the Australia gold rush. When he returned, he married Jane Cunningham and they settled at Bayhead on what became known as Clark's Point. They had five children. In 1872, James was appointed a Justice of the Peace, the first of three generations of his family to hold the position until 1934.

3) John also left Tatamagouche, with his brother James, for four years in Australia. When he returned, he married Agnes Bell and they had four children, Geordie, Gavin, John and Gordon. He eventually owned and operated a general store on Main Street and lived on the farm where the Balmoral Motel is now located. For many years he was Superintendent of the village Sunday School. He met a sudden death by drowning while swimming in the river below his house.

4) George married Agnes Aitcheson and they had seven children. After Agnes died, George married Elizabeth Cunningham and they also had seven children. George's career has already been described earlier in this book.

5) Charles got his first job with William Campbell as head farmer of the Campbell estate. Charles married Margaret Aitcheson, one of eleven Aitcheson sisters. Their children were: 1. Alexander, (m. Mary Jane Johnson); 2. Mary Jane (m. John Lombard, Alexander MacEachern): 3. Aitcheson, (m. Mary Emma Lombard); 4. Fanny, (m. Duncan MacIntosh); 5. Agnes, (m. Charles MacEachern); 6. Henry, (m. Henrietta MacEachern); 7. Charles, (m. Cassie MacKenzie). More has been written about my great grandparents, Charles and Margaret, in other parts of this narrative.

6) William immigrated to Tatamagouche with his parents and siblings. He travelled extensively to gold rushes in Nevada, California and British Columbia. Eventually he came back to Tatamagouche to look after his parents on the farm in Millbrook. He married Hannah Weatherbie and they had six children: Nettie, William, Lawrence, Chester, Herbert and Lizzie.

7) Alexander too was seized by the lure of the western gold rush. Along with his brother William he sailed around Cape Horn to the West Coast. When prospecting did not work out, he worked as a mechanic and carpenter in British Columbia, but to the dismay of his family back home, "he fell in with bad company and took an easier way of life." He became an American citizen and the last ever heard of him he was working as a bartender in a hotel in Washington State.

8) Mary was the only daughter of John and Jane Clark. She married Robert Scott and they had three children. Robert

started a small store in Tatamagouche, but died suddenly of Tetanus from stepping on a rusty nail. Mary had a desperate time with three small children and had to rely on the support of her brothers. Her brother John provided her with a house where she made a meagre living boarding some of the workers who were building the new railway. Later still, with the support of her brothers, she took care of her parents in their declining years.

9) David was another son who had died in infancy, before the move to Nova Scotia.

Growing up in Tatamagouche I actually remember some of John and Jane's grandchildren who would have been the first generation of Clarks born in Tatamagouche. Aitcheson, Henry and Charlie, sons of Charles; Gordon, son of John; and, Nettie and Lawrence, children of William, were all in their senior years when I as a child would have visited them with my parents.

Gavin Clark, another son of John Junior, married Elizabeth Campbell, daughter of Archibald Campbell, and they took over the Campbell property which later became the ACTC property. Gavin died before my time, by drowning in the French River while swimming near the railway bridge. It would seem some of the Clarks fared badly with flowing water.

John was a common name in the Clark family. There was at least one John Clark in each of four generations of the family.

* * *

Back in the years before the 1950s most commercial business happened in an east or west direction. This was possibly due to that being the course of the railway line, but for the previous 150 years the shipping of freight and supplies was done by boat along the coast of the Northumberland Strait. Back in the early 1900s there was a ferry that operated several trips a day, three days a week, between the Tatamagouche wharf and the Malagash wharf.

The highway too was in much better shape between Oxford and New Glasgow than were the gravel roads that ran from Tatamagouche over the Cobequid Hills to Truro.

I vaguely remember when Main Street through the village was a gravel thoroughfare. There were wooden board sidewalks in front of the stores. It was a huge change when the street was reconstructed and paved. My first sight of heavy construction equipment was watching the large "carryall" earth movers, cutting down the surface grade for the addition of gravel and asphalt pavement. These machines were pulled or pushed by a bulldozer and had a scraper blade underneath that dug into the road surface and forced the earth up into the open body of the machine. The load could then be transported to an area where the fill was needed.

Once it became easier to travel longer distances again after the war, and whenever my grandparents came by car from Annapolis, it seemed that there would be a family shopping trip arranged to New Glasgow. When my mother would need a new dress, or one or the other of us would need some article of good clothing, the

Goodman's department store in New Glasgow would be our
destination. The other alternative, and this would be considered a
major excursion, would be to go to the Eaton's department store in
Moncton. What I remember about my first trip there was that we ate
lunch in the store cafeteria. What would have made this so
memorable was the experience of eating in a restaurant. Previously
we always packed a picnic lunch anywhere we ever went. We
normally would not have been able to afford to eat in a restaurant,
which were few and far between anyway.

* * *

With the end of the war, veterans began to return home to the local
area. Some were injured in body and mind. What is known as PTSD
nowadays was then called "shell shock." At least one soldier brought
home a Dutch wife. I remember a victory parade at some point in
time that raised considerable comment from certain pious residents
of the village due to several of the veterans getting drunk and
becoming a bit disorderly in their celebrations.

In the years following the end of the war, the Tatamagouche
Creamery was probably the largest employer in the area. In addition
to the facility itself, which was known for making butter, the
Creamery operated a feed store and a fleet of trucks that travelled
throughout North Colchester to pick up cans of cream from the
farmers, and to deliver cattle feed and ice. Some of the men I
remember who worked at the creamery were: J.J. Creighton, owner;
Alex MacBain, accountant; Ian Creighton; Wes MacLennan, chemist;

Bill Ward, stationary engineer; Willis Bonnyman, buttermaker; Earl Langille; Cecil Langille; Arnold MacLennan; and Stewart Bonnyman.

* * *

It was about this time that I saw my first movie. I believe it was a Walt Disney production called *Fun and Fancy Free* that was partly animated. Davy Bell had a new car so he and his wife Janie invited my mother, father and me to go with them to see the movie at the Capital theatre in Truro. I got carsick on the drive over the mountain from Tatamagouche. At that time, we would have travelled what was called the new Truro Road through East New Annan, past the silica plant at Rhude's Pond, and on through MacCallum's Settlement to Truro. My car sickness was blamed on the fact that the trip to Truro in the new car was made in the fast time of one hour. Nevertheless, this did not detract from me being in awe of that movie experience, and it was the beginning of a love for movies that extended through the rest of my school years.

Another movie which was memorable in those early times was *Wizard of Oz*, including the song "Somewhere Over The Rainbow", sung by Judy Garland. Other movies starred Shirley Temple.

It was shortly after the end of the war that Rocky Hazel came to Tatamagouche and built the Rialto Theatre on Main Street, the building that has since become the Needs Store up from Big Al's Restaurant. Movies soon became a favorite source of entertainment, and the theatre lasted until television came along in the mid 1950s. Each evening's movie was accompanied by the showing of a news reel. My family enjoyed all of the song and dance movies, such as "Singing in the Rain", with Fred Astaire, Ginger Rogers and Gene Kelly.

Other favorite movies of mine over the years were: "From Here to Eternity" with Burt Lancaster, Deborah Kerr and Frank Sinatra; "Rebel Without a Cause", with James Dean and Natalie Wood; "High Society", with Bing Crosby and Grace Kelly; and, "Roman Holiday", with Gregory Peck and Audrey Hepburn. I would have seen these motion pictures when they were first released to theatres.

Movies at the Rialto theatre usually played two nights in a row and the theatre was open six nights a week, being closed on Sundays. Sometimes there would be a "double feature" where there would be two shorter films shown. There would also be a matinee on Saturday afternoon, which was popular with student-aged youth. The matinee usually included a ten-minute cartoon featuring a character such as the Roadrunner or Daffy Duck. On at least one occasion close to the end of the Rialto's lifetime, there was a showing of a new innovation in motion pictures - a 3-D film. The theatre was packed and everyone was issued a pair of cardboard eyeglasses where the plastic sight pane for one eye was red and the other was blue. Wearing these eyepieces made the movie appear to be three dimensional. I remember everyone ducking in their seats as a pitched baseball seemed to come right out of the screen into the audience.

The films for the movies came on circular reels and it was not unusual for the film strip to break or another projector malfunction to happen during a critical scene. The audience then had to sit more or less patiently while the projectionist made the necessary repairs.

* * *

Tatamagouche always had its share of interesting characters. Frank Patterson wrote in one of his books about Stewart Kisslepaugh, a well known and comical merchant in the village in the mid 1800s. In the mid 1900s, there were two other individuals who come to mind. Russell was a man who lived in a tiny house back toward the village from the Willow Church Road. Russ suffered from a serious speech impediment. He had once owned a Whippit car, which he referred to in later life as "Dat Dod Damned Dippit". Elmer was another friendly individual who, though he was afflicted with some challenges, happily roamed the village most days, greeting all who stopped to chat. At some point following the end of the war, Elmer obtained a war surplus military uniform, which then became his standard mode of everyday dress. He also acquired several war service medals which were added to the uniform. Most village residents who knew Elmer paid little attention to his garb and gear, but once in a while a veteran unfamiliar with Elmer's situation would take exception to his wearing of the medals.

Jake was another character who lived on the adjoining property to the elementary school while I was in the lower grades. When I first started school, a large, mysterious old house was still standing in the woods of that property to the north of Blair Avenue. I think it had been empty for some time, and had fallen into bad repair. The house had been built by Robert Purves, a storeowner and shipbuilder many years before. Purves had named the house "Oak Hall" and it was unique in its design. I believe Jake may have been the caretaker for the property. The extensive property was for the most part thickly wooded land between Blair Avenue and Church Street. Jake had a Russian sounding name, smoked a large cigar, wore a European style cap and I think sported a greyish beard. There were quiet suspicions circulating that Jake had been a foreign spy during the war. As kids, we were not allowed to play in these woods, which added another layer of intrigue to our young minds. We fabricated the imaginary story that there was a secret tunnel leading from the old house to some hidden exit deep in the woods. Some of us wished to explore those woods, but the spectre of Jake, possibly emerging from a hole in the ground was a strong deterrent.

In the 1950s the village of Tatamagouche really came to life on Saturday nights. Saturday was the end of the six-day work week and virtually everyone from near and far came to town to get their next week's groceries and to socialize. Cars would be parked bumper to bumper up and down both sides of the street from the community hall at the west end to the Rialto Theater on the east. Stores would stay open until at least ten o'clock and even longer if potential customers were still lingering. From personal experience during my short work term clerking at the Bonnyman and Bell General Store, there was not a moment's break from checking out the groceries for people who were buying their week's supply.

I probably should mention the politics of those times, although I had little exposure or knowledge of what was happening in that regard. My father had no interest that I am aware of in any political party other than at the time he was to be awarded the contract to build a new Post Office. One thing about politics in those days was that government jobs were only doled out to supporters of the ruling political party. If the party in power happened to be voted out at election time there was apt to be a major shakeup of employees in the various departments of government, most visibly in the Department of Highways.

It was common practice on voting day for both parties to have their support workers going to the doors of potential voters with a box of groceries or a bottle of rum as an incentive to vote for that particular party. There was one anecdote I remember of a case where that action backfired. Naturally, the boxes of groceries had to be obtained from a grocery store. At the only store in a large rural area east of the village, the owners were very strong supporters of the Progressive Conservative Party. But being the only store within a reasonable distance, the Liberals also had to obtain their gift boxes of groceries from that store. Undiscovered for some time was the fact that when the store owners packed the boxes of groceries for the Liberals, they carefully included their Tory party's literature in the bottom of the box.

* * *

At some time during my elementary school years there was a Mi'kmaq family who came to the area and lived for some time just to the west of the village. The family would travel door to door selling handmade baskets. I remember encountering the family once when I was walking home from school as they were cutting young alder trees along the roadside. In conversation they told me that they would strip the bark off the Alder sticks and salvage the inner filament between the outer bark and the wood, and use this inner bark to make medicine. Apparently, this resulting medication was used as a pain remedy similar to how we would use Aspirin today.

There were a couple of other times when Mi'kmaq people would visit the area to collect birch bark. I have seen White Birch trees at our woodlot where large strips of the bark had been removed.

* * *

When I was growing up, little thought was ever given to conservation or the natural environment. The air was always clear and fresh smelling. Pollution was not an issue. Most garbage was burned in woodstoves, contributing to heat in the house, or in garbage barrels outside. Non-flammables such as tin cans or non-reusable glass bottles could be taken to a small village landfill site on the New Truro Road. Anyone with indoor plumbing and bathroom had their own septic tank and sewage disposal system, where any outflow would be absorbed into the ground. Brooks and rivers flowed with clean water and *e. coli* was not a consideration.

Back in the 1940's there were lots of songbirds in the spring and summer. The hayfields were alive with robins, bobolinks, various types of sparrows, red winged blackbirds and a variety of others. Just before dusk could be heard the unique calls of the flock of Hungarian partridge that lived around the grain fields. There were very few crows though, and the occasional one we did see at a distance was very wary of humans. This was all before the forest spraying of DDT, which had such a devastating effect on the song bird population.

Bears in the wild were virtually unheard of when I was a kid, and this was long before the coyotes arrived in the province. This was also before there were mourning doves and cardinals, which I believe have moved northward in recent years because of milder winters. I remember seeing a large moose wander through our hayfield east of the house. Pheasants and white tail deer that are so common now are imports, not native species to the province.

At one time in the 1940s we had an infestation of bats in the attic of the house. They had discovered an entrance hole at a spot under the eaves and proceeded to develop a huge colony of bats inside the warm, unused attic space. Back then we did not know how useful bats were at controlling the mosquito population around the farm. But the smell of the bat population was beginning to permeate the upper floor of the house and there was concern that other problems might develop.

To solve the attic bat problem, my innovative father devised a trap to catch the bats exiting their daytime sanctuary. He built a stand under the exit hole to support a double boiler partially filled with water, with a baffle that deflected the bat into the water as it first took flight coming out of the attic. He got more than fifty bats that one night, and once the entrance hole was plugged, our bat problem seemed to be solved.

* * *

The village of Tatamagouche always seemed to have a huge amount of community spirit for such a small population. I believe it was more than simply a sign of the times that people were willing to pull together and volunteer for projects for the betterment of the greater community.

One of the most notable examples of the community working together happened in the mid 1950s with the holding of the Nova Scotia Festival of the Arts. This was an enormous undertaking by the citizens of the village and immediate area. One has only to look at one of the picture postcards that can still be seen on eBay to realize the amount of effort that was needed to put up all the tents, stages and prepare the food required to cater to close to 10,000 attendees. It seemed that everyone was involved in some way. I remember my father helping to pitch tents, and I had some small task that involved passing out the dated pinbacks that signified admission to the community field where many of the arts events took place.

There were many arts related activities that took place over a one-week period, from displays to demonstrations to concerts in the high school auditorium. I particularly remember the live performances of the Buchta Dancers, who we felt we knew personally from watching them on the Dom Messer Show on TV. There was also highland dancing, vocal concerts, art displays and a myriad of other activities across the full spectrum of the Arts.

Whether on account of the Festival becoming too large a project for the community, or someone in authority deciding that it needed to be closer to a larger population, the Festival was relocated to Halifax after several years of success in Tatamagouche. Unfortunately, the Festival seemed to wither away from that time forward, perhaps from the lack of volunteer support it had been given in Tatamagouche.

* * *

When I was in elementary school, Tatamagouche had its own annual Music Festival with piano and voice participants competing from across Northern Nova Scotia. It was held in Sharon United Church over a two- or three-day period of time and was well attended. Each school classroom was expected to sing in the school competitive classes. I did not compete individually, not having taken either voice or piano lessons, but I did attend the music festival sessions just to hear the music that others were making.

Anne Murray would have been one of the young voice performers at that music festival. Although Anne lived in Springhill, her grandparents lived in Tatamagouche, and Anne took voice lessons for a time from the United Church Minister's wife in Tatamagouche, who was a vocal teacher. Anne and her cousin as teenagers would often sing in the Sharon Church choir when they were visiting with their grandparents in Tatamagouche.

In the 1940s, before the establishment of a village library, a number of the local women belonged to a loosely organized "Book Club." Mrs. R.B. Fraser seemed to have held the leadership role, but my mother and a number of other women were involved. I am not sure how the club worked, but wished-for book titles would be chosen, money collected, and Mrs. Fraser would place an order to a publisher/distributer for the books, which would eventually be delivered to her to be shared out to readers.

* * *

My memory is a bit hazy on this one, but Sharon United had a church hall located between the back of the church and where the fire station is located now. At some time in the 1940s, the hall was purchased by Frank Buckler and moved to Frank's property on the west side of Main Street where the Foodland Mall parking lot is now. Frank converted the building for use in his farm equipment supply business, which he operated to the east of his residence. Back from there toward the village, Miss Janie Powers had a little shop on the corner of Park Street where she sold needles, thread and other sewing supplies.

The Balmoral Motel is located now on the opposite side of Main Street on what was then the farm of Gordon Clark and his son Hallie. Gordon had operated a general store in the main business section of Main Street and at one time raised silver foxes on the farm property. Hallie was a bachelor who worked at odd jobs and sometimes helped my father make hay in the summertime.

In the years before the present fire hall was built, many community events were held in the community hall, commonly referred to as the "town hall" on the north side of Main Street opposite Sharon United Church. This building was used generally for card parties, school concerts, dances, youth group activities, charity suppers, etc. I do not think I ever saw it, but there was reputed to be a jail cell in the basement of the town hall. I do have a mental image but suspect that image may have been instilled in us as school children as a deterrent not to misbehave.

In the early 1940s Santa Claus would make an annual visit to the community hall on Christmas Eve day. All of the younger kids in the village would wait with impatient anticipation inside the hall for Santa to arrive. There would be a great commotion when he showed up with a bulky burlap bag over his shoulder. The sack would be full of small paper bags (each containing an orange and assorted pieces of hard candy) that would be passed out all around. It was an exciting time. Back then we didn't recognize the faint odour of alcohol on Santa's breath.

Musical performances back in those times included so many of the wartime songs that are still so familiar to some of us today. They were beautiful songs with words that told a story and actually meant something to those involved in the war efforts. Songs like "The White Cliffs of Dover," "A Nightingale Sang in Berkley Square," "Lilly Marlene," and "It's a Long Way to Tipperary," that have become classic representatives of the music of those times.

It was commonplace for variety concerts to include skits and musical selections in blackface. This was only thought of then as musical entertainment, no different than an actor in costume as a performer in a play.

On a number of occasions plays would be performed with local residents taking on the various roles. I have a program for one such three-act play directed by Mrs. G.E. Whidden, in which Hattie Langille, Jennie Fulton, Wm. B. Nelson, Alex MacBain, John Swan and Arnold MacLennan were cast members.

Someone who had the greatest impact on the cultural life of Tatamagouche, spanning decades, was Dr. Elizabeth (Betty) Murray. Betty was the daughter of Dr. Dan Murray and his wife Morna, and she grew up in the village. After graduating from the Provincial Normal College and Mount Allison University, she began her teaching career in 1940, in the one room "Tarbet" school in Barrachois. Her method of teaching was unique in that she concentrated as much on creating knowledge of useful life skills as on teaching the three R's. In those early years she organized operettas, such as the Gilbert and Sullivan plays, at Tatamagouche. She went on to employment with the Adult Education Division of the provincial Department of Education where she was a driving force in the promotion of the Arts across the Province. Later in her career, she was a playwright who created a series of performances on the history of Tatamagouche, was the founder of the Tatamagouche and Area Choir, and was one of the primary movers in the establishment of the Festival of the Arts at Tatamagouche. She was eventually awarded an honorary doctorate by Acadia University. Betty was a fierce promoter of the Arts, and also of her home community of Tatamagouche. I remember of being scolded by Betty because in a letter attributed to me it was stated that I was born in Middleton and she chastised me that it should have said that I was native of Tatamagouche.

On the Dominion Day and Labour Day holidays there would usually be an afternoon baseball game on the community ball field, followed by a baked bean with brown bread or ham with potato scallop fundraising supper held in the community hall. My mother and many of the women in the village would be busy cooking beforehand, and later serving at the supper. Rows of tables would be set up the length of the hall and people would sit wherever a spot became available. Servers would quickly arrive with plates of food followed by others with white enamel pitchers of hot tea.

The community hall was the venue for the annual village flower show, which was a major late summer event back in the 1940s. The flower show was a single event, held in the village, as sort of a local version of the regional flower and vegetable competitions that are components of the county exhibitions. At the Tatamagouche Flower Show there was quite a rivalry amongst a number of the village ladies as to who could enter the most prizewinning examples of different varieties of flowers, fruits and vegetables. There was a section of the show for children's entries and I won several prizes myself for my displays of wild flowers. My mother was involved with the local Garden Club and I believe she was the flower show coordinator one year.

My mother always had an extensive flower garden each summer at the farm. For several years she and Jennie Fulton looked after the placing of flowers in Sharon United for the Sunday morning services. It was a Saturday night ritual for them to go through her garden to round up appropriate bouquets of flowers to take to the church and arrange them to suit. There was one other sometime member of the flower committee, who will remain anonymous, who on one occasion disagreed with the colour of the chosen flowers, an action which required some difficult negotiation to come up with a suitable replacement.

Once the new fire hall began to be used for more community events, the old town hall was sold to Tommy Pugh, where for a number of years he operated a war surplus store.

* * *

Another prominent event, held once in Tatamagouche in the late 1940s, was a provincial Plowing Match. It was held at the Lombard farm in the twenty plus acre field directly across the road from our farm. This turned out to be quite an event with a large crowd of people attending from near and far. Narrow strips or sections were staked out across the field with one strip allotted for each contestant. There were different categories for the use of tractors or horses. The object was to plough your section in straight lines with each furrow turned over in the most presentable manner. I think Earle's motive for hosting the competition was to get his field ploughed for free, but some contestants were not as capable as others and Earle ended up having to do a great deal of tidying up afterward.

* * *

Between 1954 and 1956 the Atlantic Christian Training Centre was established on land purchased on the north side of the mouth of the French River. This land had for many years been owned by Alexander Campbell and his heirs, being the location of the extensive Campbell shipbuilding works. After the demise of the shipbuilding industry the property was farmed by Gavin (Buzz) Clark and later used as a campground by a series of tourism operators.

The ACTC soon became a busy centre for leadership training and other religious activities for the United Church of Canada. I can remember participating in several church youth group meetings and Allied Youth socials with other teenagers from across the province during the first year or so, these events being held in the old farmhouse that had come with the property.

Back in those days the Route #6 Highway bordered the ACTC, and the entrance to the training centre was on the sharp corner leading down to the old Campbell's Bridge. This was an extremely dangerous section of highway with many accidents over the years. Cars coming from the direction of Bayhead had little warning of the 90-degree corner and, if going too fast to navigate the curve, there was danger of going over the edge of the steep bank and down toward the river. The screech of car brakes was a common sound in that area.

Above Campbell's Bridge and directly across the highway from the ACTC property was the home of Mrs. Crowe. Mrs. Crowe was an elderly woman whom I remember visiting as a child when my mother made one of her social "calls" to drop in for tea. Mrs. Crowe seemed to be a person my mother visited quite regularly, for Mrs. Crowe once sent a couple of oranges back home to me as a special treat. My father also did odd carpentry jobs for Mrs. Crowe. I believe she may have been a daughter of one of the last Campbell shipbuilders. In my mother's 1945 diary she mentions that she attended a sale in mid August of Mrs. Crowe's books and paintings and that Charlie ended up crating Mrs. Crowe's furniture to go to the Pattersons.

On the opposite side of Campbell's Bridge, on the curved highway leading to the crest of the hill and the village, was located a popular spring of drinking water. A pipe came out of the roadside river bank with clear cold water flowing into a concrete water trough. This spring was a popular stopping spot for a cool drink on a hot day and

I expect it would have been used in earlier days as a place to water horses for someone coming from the direction of Bayhead.

On the north side of the highway and directly across the river from the ACTC was the Patterson property. There is a lot of history associated with this plot of land too, but I will leave that to someone else better versed in shipbuilding history than I am. When I was a youngster, however, this was the home of the Patterson family. Frank H. Patterson was a prominent lawyer in Truro and had authored several books of historical significance pertaining to Tatamagouche and area. At that time, he was the reigning expert on what had gone on in the previous century. In later years, once Judge Patterson had retired, I was able to meet with him on several occasions and learned more about the early Langille and Tattrie settlers along the French River intervale land in the area of our farm and the Donaldson Bridge.

At one of my meetings with Judge Patterson he presented me with a copper nugget that he had had in his possession. It had been produced by the copper mining operations of an earlier era on the Waugh River. This nugget probably originally come from the mine located on "Mine Hole Brook," just to the east of the present Route 311. It may even have been a souvenir from the ship loaded with copper that sank in Tatamagouche Harbour.

Opposite the Patterson property, on the northwest corner of the Lake Road/Main Street intersection, was the home of Miss Georgia Spinney and her sister and brother. The family appeared to me in my youth to be elderly and all three unmarried. Miss Spinney had a beautiful flower garden, from which (according to my mother's early 1940s diary) Miss Spinney often supplied the flowers to decorate Sharon United Church for Sunday worship services.

A couple of my schoolmates, who lived nearby, Clayton Langille and Carson Tattrie, did odd jobs for the Spinney and Patterson families. Carson worked for the Pattersons and Clayton for Miss Spinney. I think I may have been a bit envious as both the Pattersons and Miss Spinney were reputed to be very generous with their financial compensation for the work efforts of the boys.

Back to the ACTC landsite itself this parcel of land holds much of historical significance. It was the location of the northern part of the Acadian village of Tatamagouche, and was the very first site from whence the Expulsion of the Acadians began on August 15, 1755.

Bordering on the north side of the ACTC property is an old cemetery, which was used by the Montbeliard settlers in the late 1700s. I understand that this early burial ground has all but disappeared over the passage of time and the vagaries of shoreline erosion.

I feel it is very unfortunate that little recognition has been given to the significant events in the history of the Tatamagouche that have occurred in the areas at the mouth of the French River. There is an opportunity here that it is hoped the powers-that-be will recognize and promote. Given the popularity of the Grand Pre historical site, perhaps the village commissioners could develop some plan to promote Tatamagouche as an historical destination for tourists.

CHAPTER 8 - CHANGES

In the years following the end of the war, huge lifestyle changes began to take place. The economy improved, more paid employment became available, and money began to circulate, which stimulated an improved lifestyle. This time period saw a large number of changes that improved the way we lived on the farm.

Having gotten electrical service early in the war years meant that as more money became available, other lifestyle changes could begin to take place. Because of the distance between farms on the Lake Road, the power company had balked at installing a new power line from the village. Electric power at that time was supplied by the Northumberland Light and Power Company, with the electricity generated from the hydro dam at The Falls. My father, Earl Lombard and Davy Bell made an agreement with Bill Langille, who had his slaughter house located just east of the present-day substation, that they would help him wire the slaughterhouse so the power company would have the required number of customers on the Lake Road to make the distance work.

A Mr. Ross did the wiring of our house and my uncle Bill Ward wired the barn a year or so later. As a Stationary Engineer and all-round maintenance man at the Tatamagouche Creamery, Uncle Bill was knowledgeable with electricity and he did a good job. Once we had electricity, the next thing was to have a drilled well for running water.

I remember that before the well was drilled my father had someone come to the farm who was known to be able to "witch" for the location where water could be found. This man used a forked stick, part of a branch from an apple tree. He walked in lines back and forth across the yard holding the two prongs of the witching stick horizontally, one in each hand turned so the back of each hand faced up, until the point of the stick was drawn to point downward, supposedly to where a seam of water was located. Finally, after several test circuits across the yard the witching stick settled on a location close to the north side of the house foundation.

The well was drilled by Ernie MacDonald, father of Ken MacDonald, NSLS. Luckily, water was struck at a relatively shallow depth, and was tested to be soft and suitable for drinking. A water line was run underground to the barn so that the cattle could have water bowls beside their stanchions. This saved the work of watering the cows by hand. Until then, this had been accomplished by bailing water out of the rock lined dug well with a pail, pouring it into a trough outdoors and letting the cows out to exercise and drink.

The addition of a milking machine meant that more cows could be milked. The milking machine was a huge labour saver in that each cow did not have to be milked by hand twice a day. Before that the job required one to sit next to the side of the cow on a low stool, with a milk pail between one's knees and with each hand on a teat, alternately squeezing and pulling to direct the streams of milk into the pail.

After the war years my father began to improve the quality of the herd. He often attended meetings of Jersey cow cream producers. He interbred some Guernsey cows into the herd mix to increase milk production. For a number of years he kept a bull to breed our own cows and the cows of other neighbouring farmers who did not own a bull of their own.

We kept a sow pig for several years in order to produce litters of young piglets ourselves. This turned out to be less than successful. To begin with we did not have a boar pig so the sow would have to be transported to Johnny Ferguson's farm in Bayhead for a few days' honeymoon to be bred there. Then when the litter arrived the sow was apt to lay down on one or two of the little ones and suffocate them. Eventually, we purchased the young weaned pigs directly from Johnny Ferguson or another pig farmer in the area.

The new well was drilled in 1945 but it was not until the winter of 1946 that we finally got running water in the house and barn. By then, my sister was taking her Grade 12 at school in Annapolis Royal, so her vacant bedroom at home was converted into a bathroom with the installation of a sink, toilet and bathtub. Tommy Simpson did all the plumbing to install the water pump, kitchen sink and bathroom fixtures. Tommy worked on a slightly different workday schedule. He used to come in the afternoon or early evening and work until one or two o'clock in the morning.

It seemed during this period that money gradually became more available to buy necessities. My father expanded the barn and added a few more cows and started to raise more pigs. This of course added more work around the farm, and my father had to cut back on his carpentry jobs for customers in the village. The sale of cream and pork became the chief sources of income from the farm. Once the pigs reached a certain size, they were taken to the rail station in Tatamagouche, tattooed with an identification number, and loaded on a railcar with others to go to a meat packing plant in Moncton to be slaughtered.

With electricity we were also able to purchase a refrigerator. This appliance was bought from Frank Buckler who sold refrigerators as a sideline to his International Harvester farm equipment business. Several other electrical appliances came into common use in the house. My mother was given an electric coffee percolator by my grandparents and thereafter coffee often became the beverage of choice over tea, especially when there was company. Our first electric toaster was the model where the sides folded down to put the bread in, then a close watch had to be kept to prevent the toast from burning. Automatic it was not.

Each year for several years I was given ownership of a baby pig. In return I was to help feed the herd, clean the pens, and do other barn chores. Once the pig was raised and sent to market, I usually received from $15 to $25 for my pig. The pig was in lieu of an allowance.

One of my other chores was to go get the cows from the pasture and herd them into the barn for the evening milking. The pasture was all along the half mile of so of river hillside and the cows would range over the whole area throughout the day. Sometimes I had to travel a fair distance to find them if they happened to be down by the marsh at milking time. The alpha cow usually had a bell so that if the cow was moving, I could hear the bell and know where to find them. There was a hierarchy within the herd and they followed a bit of a pecking order on the way to the barn and to their own stanchions inside. One thing I learned was that cows are not the smartest animals in the barnyard. Pigs, given the opportunity, are much more intelligent and keep themselves much cleaner than cattle.

Each summer for a number of years we raised several dozen roosters. Early each spring my mother would order day-old chicks from the J&J Proudfoot chick hatchery in New Glasgow. On the appointed delivery date, the chicks would arrive by train, loose in a large cardboard container. Since they had just hatched the chicks would be taken into the kitchen for warmth (still in their container) and they would be given chick starter food, and water, to get them started on eating. They would stay in the house for a period of time until they were old enough to survive outdoors in the wire chicken coop out behind the barn. Once they were big enough, they were let loose in the daytime to forage for food around the barnyard area. I was responsible for feeding the roosters and making sure they were all locked up in their coop at night so foxes would not catch and kill them.

Come fall the birds would weigh about seven or eight pounds each. My mother would start taking orders to sell the dressed roosters to her friends in the village. This was her source of Christmas money. When she received a request for a chicken there was a fair bit of work involved. The roosters by then were a bit on the wild side so we first had to catch one. We had an actual catching tool, a long-handled metal hook designed to snag the chicken by the leg and hold it. Next step was the axe and chopping block to lop off the bird's head. Killing the rooster in this manner meant it bled properly to ensure that the meat was not bloody. Plucking the feathers was the worst. By quickly dipping the dead bird in scalding water the feathers came out much easier without tearing the skin. The smell however, was gag worthy, seeming to be many times worse than the smell of a wet dog. The bird would then be cleaned and dressed, the liver, gizzard and heart would be put back inside, and it would be ready for delivery.

Once, in the middle of the night, a fox got into the chicken coop somehow. It caught and bit the heads off about eight of the full-grown roosters. The commotion of the frightened fowl must have woken my father so he rushed outdoors in his bare feet and after letting the dog loose gave chase to the fox. Running with the dog, in his bare feet, oblivious to the rough ground and stubble field, they eventually cornered the fox and my father killed it with a rock. Only after the adrenaline rush of the chase was over did Dad notice the scratches and bruises to his bare feet.

Losing the revenue from the sale of the roosters would have been heartbreaking to my mother. It turned out though that the fox had only had time to kill the birds and had not damaged them otherwise. With the heads bitten off they had all bled properly. Thus it was that we spent the next day plucking and dressing the birds, and my mother was able to sell most of them to her customers in the village. She may not have mentioned the manner in which the birds had met their demise.

At the end of the war years the Canadian government instituted a program that was a godsend to families with young children. This was the beginning of the Family Allowance program, or what was commonly referred to as the "baby bonus." Under this program a government cheque for an amount from $5 to $8 dollars would arrive in the mail each month to mothers of children under 16 years of age. The day of the baby bonus cheque's arrival was looked forward to with great anticipation in every household. The amount may not seem like much nowadays but in those times the money went a long way in providing food and clothing for a family of young children.

* * *

I never had very good luck with pets. A couple of times in my early life we had a dog and at one stage one of them was mine. I named him Mickey. Unfortunately, every time a car would go by on the Lake Road the dog would run out the lane to give chase. We were unable to break the dog of this habit. Even though there was not much traffic going by, one day the dog actually caught up to a car and it ended up being run over and killed. That was the last dog we had on the farm. We always had cats too, but they were barn cats to control the mice, and neither the dog nor the cats were ever allowed in the house.

At one stage I thought it would be fun to raise ducks. After some negotiating, we were able to purchase a pair of domestic ducks from someone who owned a flock of ducks in Bible Hill. I dammed up the drainage ditch that runs to the east of the barn to create a small pond for my ducks. Come spring the female began laying an egg every day or so in a nest I created in a corner of the shed. I guess she was not in a very maternal mood that spring, for only two of the eggs ever hatched.

Growing up on a farm, one learns not to become too attached to any particular animal. Pigs and calves could almost have become pets, but this would have been unwise when the animal's end purpose was to be sold to be slaughtered. Male calves were killed shortly after they were born because there was no market for them. It is a fact of life that animals and birds are slaughtered to provide us with food. Therefore, I think that by living on a farm, one develops a more open-minded perspective about life and death.

* * *

In the mid 1940s my father was selling some of the cream to Miss Margaret Patterson, who then operated the Lynwood Inn on the village waterfront. The Lynwood was advertised as having six bedrooms, one bathroom and salt water bathing.

The Lynwood was located on the harbour side of Main Street, close to the railway. The hillside between the inn and Main Street was then all open cow pasture. One way to reach the Inn was via the narrow street that ran down to the public wharf, which is now called King Street. Then as now there was a steep drop off from the side of Main Street. On one trip to deliver cream to the Inn I was along for the ride, in the back seat of the car along with the can containing a couple of gallons of cream. It was wintertime and there was ice everywhere. Somehow the car missed the turn and went down over the embankment. The car remained upright in its journey down into the pasture, but the cream can upset and there was spilled cream everywhere in the back seat and floor of the car. I was not hurt, but I remember that my father was much more concerned at the financial loss of the cream than he was about checking to see if I was hurt.

My mother also had a little sideline where she supplied eggs and cream and vegetables to some of her friends in the village. I don't think much money actually changed hands as the women would have reciprocated in other ways. In my mother's diary, however, she did mention selling corn and celery to both meat markets in the village. One such 1942 entry indicated she sold six dozen ears of corn to Will MacQueen's market for twenty-five cents a dozen.

Sometime shortly after the end of the war the old car was traded in for a new Chevrolet half ton pickup truck. The truck was bought at Langille Bros Chevrolet Oldsmobile dealership on Main Street, owned by Roy and Ells Langille. My father did a lot of dickering with the two Langille brothers to get the best price he could on that deal.

Buying the truck was another huge turning point in our lifestyle. Having a reliable vehicle meant that it was possible to get to the village any time there was a need, and our family could travel farther afield. Raising more pigs meant that there was usually a trip with the truck to the Tatamagouche Creamery each day to get buttermilk. My father had mounted an old wooden molasses puncheon on the back of the truck to haul the buttermilk home to feed the pigs. Buttermilk is a byproduct of making butter, and the creamery sold it for fifty cents a barrel. This trip also meant that I usually had a ride to school in the morning.

The truck would also have been used to take "a grist" down to the feed mill at the creamery. A grist was several bags of grain grown at the farm and taken to a mill to be roughly ground, then brought back home and used as a feed supplement for the cattle and poultry.

The disadvantage of the truck was that it really only held three people comfortably in the cab. It had a bench style seat so four people could squeeze in, but when my parents had someone else along, I was usually relegated to the back of the truck. My father even built a wood frame, canvas covered box or cap for the back of the truck, which was weatherproof in a rainstorm. Dave Lombard and I took a number of trips in the back of the truck. Earl Lombard also had a half ton truck, a Studebaker, but his did not have a cap on the back. Earl chewed tobacco and spit the tobacco juice out his side window while driving. With the wind stream carrying the juice around behind the cab, it was not so pleasant travelling in the back of Earl's truck.

* * *

So many changes meant the farm had to become more productive, or maybe it was the need to be more productive that meant more changes had to be made. Sharing a tractor was no longer feasible. It went from three owners to two and finally in 1953 we bought our own Ferguson tractor. This then required converting the drawbars on the old horse-drawn hay mowing machine and the old grain binder so they could be pulled by the tractor. We also ended up buying a side delivery rake and hay loader to mechanize. My father built a two-wheeled cart to replace the four-wheeled horse-drawn wagon used to haul hay.

I learned to drive a tractor when I was ten years old, probably as soon as my legs were long enough to reach the clutch and brake pedals safely. Thus, in springtime I drove the tractor to harrow the fields to prepare for planting the oats and barley. In summer I drove the tractor to haul in hay. My father and Earl Lombard still shared ownership of the haying equipment, so both farms worked together to make the hay. Earl still used a four-wheeled wagon so I had to learn to back up one of those with the tractor to get the loads of hay into the barns. There was a lot of skill required to back up a wagon with a tractor, a skill I mastered much better than Earl himself.

Dave Lombard was my age and being at the Lombard farm every day in the summer, the two of us each drove a tractor during haying season. Once a load of hay was backed onto the barn floor it had to be unloaded. This process involved driving a large hay fork down into the top of the wagon load of hay. The fork had hooks on the tongs, and once the fork was imbedded deeply enough in the hay load the hooks were locked. Then with a system of rope, pulleys, and track along the inside of the barn roof, about a quarter of the load could be lifted up and dumped into the haymow by pulling the rope with the tractor. We were paid ten cents per load of hay that we helped unload in the barn.

Dave and I also made a bit of money mowing the lawns at both farms. We roughly divided each lawn in half and each of us would mow one half, alternating halves every other time to be fair. At that time each place had a push mower and we were paid fifty cents per lawn.

There were of course other farm tasks that were not as appealing as driving the tractor. The worst job on the farm in my mind was picking rocks off the fields in the spring in preparation to planting grain. This was an exercise where we would drive back and forth across a harrowed field and stoop to pick any rocks more than a couple of inches in size and throw then into the dump cart. I'm not sure if it was because this was such a boring manual task, but I hated picking rocks.

Another unpleasant farm task was to spread manure in the spring. We did have a four-wheeled manure spreader that was pulled by the team of horses and later by the tractor. Back then the manure spreader had to be loaded by hand by standing on the manure pile in rubber boots and pitching forkfuls of manure into the box of the spreader. Once the load was in place it was off to the field where the manure was to be spread. The manure spreader had a seat on the front of it directly behind the horses. There was a spinning mechanism on the back of the spreader sort of like a modern snow blower in reverse that scattered the manure in a swath out the back end. The problem was that if there was a strong tailwind the driver tended to be spattered with some of the flying manure. And we did not have a shower in the house to jump into at the end of the day. Manure, especially pig manure, tends to have a long lingering aroma.

A major job each spring, as soon as the frost was out of the ground, was to upgrade the pasture fencing. Fence posts loosen in the ground as the ground thaws, so each post has to be driven back down firmly by pounding the top with a heavy post mall. Sometimes the fence wire also needed to be spliced, or the staples replaced. If the wire was loose and sagging, it would have to be tightened with a block and tackle. Wooden fence posts have to be replaced over time as they rot off just below ground level. Juniper posts last the longest of any of the local wood species, so my father always had a stock of fence posts on hand that had been cut at the woodlot with points sharpened with an axe.

* * *

The Eaton's and Simpson's catalogues back in those times were next to the Holy Bible as probably the most important works of printed material present in every household. We think of the popularity of online shopping nowadays as a product of the internet, but back then for anything other than groceries and common hardware that could be picked up locally, the popular way to shop was by searching through one the catalogues and then either placing an order by mail or placing the order through the Eaton's or Simpson's order offices, both of which were located in the village.

It was always a momentous occasion when the spring/summer or fall/winter catalogues would arrive. Many hours of enjoyment would follow over the coming months leafing through and looking at all the wondrous articles displayed. We would earmark pages that showed particular items that we wished for. We could only dream of owning most of the things, but it was so much fun to study every detail and imagine what it would be like have one of those of our own.

Items ordered from Eaton's would arrive at the order office for pickup within several days of placing an order. The regional distribution centre was in Moncton. Considering the excellent rail service at that time, one did not have to wait long for the parcel to arrive in Tatamagouche.

The Eaton's order office was located on the opposite side of Main Street, across from the present post office. There was always a display of some sort in the front window, usually a couple of manikins dressed with the latest style of women's finery. Possibly these were items of clothing that had been ordered by a customer, found to be the wrong size and returned. Rather than ship the item back to the company, the order office would display it in the window. I remember too that there was often a sheet of amber cellophane hanging just inside the window glass so that the sun did not fade the clothing while it was being displayed.

The Simpson's order office was located inside Cecil Fulton's Nyal drug store. Simpson's was eventually taken over by the Sears, Roebuck Company and the catalogue became Simpsons-Sears for a number of years, eventually becoming just Sears.

* * *

At some time in the late 1940s I was given a "View Master" stereoscope and several reels of pictures of scenery from US National Parks. View Masters became quite a fad for a time as a modern-day version of the old parlour stereoscopes. The pictures were actually coloured transparencies, which appeared in 3D in the View Master viewer. I collected picture reels over several years as Christmas and birthday gifts, then I discovered in the Eaton's catalogue that there was a View Master projector available whereby one could actually project the pictures on a white wall or even a sheet hung as a screen.

Getting one of the View Master Projectors rose to the top of my wish list. Back then everything was much less expensive if bought in the United States. As it happened, this was the year my grandparents took our family on a trip to Boston and Hartford, where we visited my father's sister Jane's family in Malden and my mother's sister Betty's family in Farmington, Connecticut. As luck would have it for me, during our visit in Boston, we all took the "Ell" (the Boston Elevated Railway) downtown and went shopping at Filene's Basement, famous for its discounted prices on all items. Lo and behold there was a View Master projector for sale for seven dollars and I had that much money saved. I made my purchase and could hardly wait to get back home so I could put on picture shows in our own house.

CHAPTER 9 - ACTIVITIES

From the time I was ten or twelve years old I earned money from trapping. Trapping season was from October 15 until the end of November. I trapped muskrats, squirrels, racoons, red foxes and mink, though mostly muskrats, which were plentiful in the marsh along the French River at the rear of the farm. When I caught any animals, I skinned them then stretched and dried the pelts, and mailed them off to Mr. E.I. Angus, a fur buyer in Amherst. Considering that wages for a workman were less than a dollar an hour, there was good money to be made from trapping. A good muskrat pelt sold for $3 to $5, and I received $15 one time for a mink pelt.

I also snared rabbits. There were lots of rabbits in the woods at the back of the Lombard farm. In the winter, if there was not too much snow on the ground, I would set snares on rabbit trails in the alder and softwood thickets. Rabbits could be sold in the village for their meat for a dollar or two per pair.

There was also a provincial bounty of fifty cents on foxes. In order to receive the bounty, one had to cut the snout off the dead animal and take it to the local forest ranger for verification.

Aside from the red foxes that are so common in Nova Scotia, in those days there were also greyish black foxes in the Tatamagouche area. I remember one running across a field that I was harrowing with the tractor. These foxes were descendants of silver foxes that had escaped their pens at the height of the earlier silver fox fur industry in the area. I was never lucky enough to trap a black fox.

I grew up with guns. My mother had a small .22 calibre rifle and I was shooting rats in the barn at a very early age. We also had a twelve-gauge shotgun that my father used to shoot ducks down on the marsh in the fall. The shotgun had quite a kick to it when fired, so I was probably fifteen or sixteen before I used it much myself. Once I was old enough, I hunted all along the hillside of the river for partridge and in the marsh for wild ducks. It was possible to sneak up on ducks feeding in the marsh by hiding behind the old Acadian dykes along the French River. I once got three partridge with one shot by patiently waiting until they were all lined up in a row.

In those time, many people (especially those living in the countryside) owned rifles or shotguns. Following the war, surplus .303 calibre army rifles were easy to obtain. On the farm, a gun was simply another work tool, used to kill rodents or to hunt for food for the table. In our house the guns were hung on hooks on the wall by the back door. Ammunition was readily available for sale at

Hayman Brothers hardware store in the village, with no age limits or permits required to purchase it.

I also had a .22 calibre, 7 shot revolver that had been my grandmother's when she lived in Wyoming. It was small, almost Derringer size, so not very accurate. I only used it for target practice at tin cans on top of a fencepost.

I shot my first two deer in the woods at the back of the Lombard farm with the shotgun, loaded with goose shot. I must have been younger than sixteen at the time because I had to get Earl Lombard to claim the deer.

The provincial Department of Lands and Forests used to hold an auction each year of guns and other items that the game wardens and police had confiscated from people convicted of illegal hunting activities. Once I was old enough, I was able to buy a 12 Gauge shotgun for my own at one of those auctions. I paid three dollars for it, and there was no sales tax in those days.

Back in those early times, wild game was an important meat supplement in our diets. There was no financial cost other than for ammunition. We ate all the game we killed. Ducks, geese, grouse and Hungarian partridge would be plucked or skinned, cleaned and then roasted. Deer would be hung for a few days then butchered into roasts, steaks and meat for mincemeat. Almost every part of a deer would be used, except for the head, hide and hooves. The deer hide could be sold to the hardware store for a couple of dollars.

During the winter, when there was lots of snow on the ground, the flocks of Hungarian partridge would burrow themselves into the soft snow to keep warm. If there was an ice storm the surface of the snow might unfortunately become covered with a crust of ice and the partridge would be unable to dig themselves out. Whenever I knew where they were located, I used to break up the crust trapping them to set them free.

Whenever there was much snow on the ground, I would throw a dipper full of milled grain on a spot on our front lawn that I could watch from the kitchen window of the house. This feed would soon attract a variety of birds with the partridge usually coming just before dusk.

In early spring, as soon as the ice was out of the French River, the smelts would make their annual run up the river to spawn. Over a period of a week, the water at the two bridges at Donaldson's would be darkened by the schools of smelts fighting their way upstream. After school each day, some of my village schoolmates and I would "jig" for smelts. Very little fishing gear was needed; just a line or strong string, several hooks and a lead sinker. We would cut an alder sapling for a pole, attach the line to the upper end, tie a couple of hooks and the sinker to the end of the line, then position ourselves on the edge of the riverbank and drop our line into the darkest part of the school of fish. No bait was needed, just the bare hooks. Once the hooks had sunk to what we deemed the proper distance we would give the pole a quick jerk upward. Most times there would be at least one smelt dangling from the hook. It was pretty easy to jig several dozen smelts in an hour that way.

Several weeks after the smelts, the gaspereau would also work their way upstream to spawn. These fish were fun to catch, also by jigging, but gaspereau are so scaly and bony that they were not considered fit to eat. Some people caught them to use as fertilizer, planting one fish alongside each seed potato in their garden.

On one of my more serious trout fishing expeditions I had my mother drop me off in Millbrook one Saturday, at the bridge on the Millbrook Road, with my intention being to fish my way down the brook to Cooper's Bridge. Little did I realize that although the distance did not appear to be long by road, the Mill Brook over that section of its course makes a series of switchback turns so that it is probably double or triple the distance to travel. I do not think my catch that day was worth the effort, but I do remember that somewhere midway in my journey downstream I came across a large piece of rock with a very obvious fossil on its surface. The fossil was the image of a large fern frond perfectly outlined on the rock surface. Unfortunately, the rock was much too heavy for me to carry with me, but later in life during my stint as a mineral prospector I wondered if there may have been other interesting fossils exposed along that section of the river. I will leave that, however, for someone else to determine.

* * *

I bought my first and only bicycle with money I earned from trapping and the sale of my pigs. It was a CCM full sized bicycle which cost $50 from MacKay's General store in the village. I probably got the bicycle when I was in Grade 5 because then I peddled it back and forth to school when the weather was good. It had a battery powered light, a bell, and a wire basket attached to the front of the handlebar to hold my book bag of school supplies.

I also used the bicycle to go to the Saturday movie matinees at the Rialto Theatre, which was on Main Street just south of where Big Al's restaurant is now. Admission was twenty-five cents. The movie was usually a Western with Roy Rogers and Dale Evans and Roy's Palomino horse "Trigger", or Gene Autry, Hopalong Cassidy, or another popular cowboy movie star of those times. If I really wanted to splurge, which I rarely did, a glass bottle of Hub ginger ale, a package of Wrigley's Juicyfruit gum, or a large Oh Henry chocolate bar were a nickel each.

One of the best parts of the Saturday matinee was the serial which was shown before the start of the main feature. The serial was about a ten-minute segment of a thriller movie that always stopped at a very tense moment in the action so we had to wait for the next segment the following Saturday to learn how the tight spot was resolved. These serials would go on for several months for each title, thus ensuring that we did not want to miss a single matinee. A couple of those serials would have been "Mysterious Island" and "Twenty Thousand Leagues Under the Sea".

* * *

My hobby during my school years was collecting postage stamps. This was an activity well suited to me when I had idle time in the evenings and no friends close enough to visit back and forth with or even to communicate with. Because everyone wrote and received letters, and one actually needed stamps to mail parcels in those days, there were always postage stamps arriving in the mail. Christmas was a bonus time for stamps with the number of Christmas cards and parcels arriving by mail. With relatives in Newfoundland and the United States there were all sorts of different stamps to collect. The cost of a stamp to mail an ordinary letter was up to four cents by then.

Stamp collecting was a great way to learn geography. Historical events were also commemorated frequently. My stamp album had a world map inside the front cover where it was possible to find the countries where different stamps originated. There was also an exposure to different world languages in the search to identify stamps when the country's name was often printed in that country's own language.

It is unfortunate that stamp collecting has since fallen by the wayside with the advent of electronic communications and courier services.

* * *

Sometime during the last of the war years, once we had electricity, my grandparents gave us an electric radio. Before that we had a large old cabinet model that was battery operated and stood in a corner of the kitchen. In order to conserve the life of the battery, the old radio was only turned on at 6 o'clock in the evening to catch the news from Station CBA in Sackville, New Brunswick. All I remember from those news broadcasts during the war years were reports of ships being sunk by the German submarines and the number of lives missing or drowned. The other thing back then was that we had to have an annual license to own the radio.

With the new electric radio, I had many hours of enjoyment in winter evenings. Besides the regular AM band with CFCY in Charlottetown and CJFX in Antigonish, this radio had a shortwave band. I learned a lot about geography from listening to shortwave radio stations all over the world.

I remember when radio station CKCL in Truro first began to transmit on the AM band. It had pretty low wattage in the beginning, so was not easy to receive clearly on our side of the Cobequid Hills.

Ham radio was a popular hobby in the 1950s. By tuning in to the twenty-metre band on the shortwave radio, I was able to listen in on the conversations of amateur radio operators across North America and Europe. I started to learn Morse Code at one point, but did not have the apparatus to practice. Many of the Ham radio transmissions were in Morse, because that was a requirement in order to obtain a Ham operator's license, and many new operators continued to communicate in that mode.

On the AM band after dusk in the winter evenings, the American AM radio stations would begin to come in loud and clear. I listened to stations WNBC and WOR in New York City because they played mostly Hit Parade music. It must have been due to atmospheric conditions that during the night I was able to pick up AM music radio stations as far away as WWVA in Wheeling, West Virginia.

Living in Tatamagouche, the radio station listened to the most was CFCY in Charlottetown, which came in loud and clear at all times, being only fifteen miles or so directly across the Northumberland Strait. CFCY played mostly Country music so my preference was to listen to the American stations that played pop music. CFCY, however, had request shows where one could write a letter to the show (anonymously) requesting a song dedication. This was a popular way to tease some of our school classmates without them knowing who made the request.

At one time in my mid teen years I received a small AM radio as a Christmas present. I managed to take the radio apart and connect a pair of war surplus aviator earphones to it so that I could listen to the radio in my room at any time of the night.

The detective programs on radio were also favorites of mine and I looked forward to listening to those half hour shows each week. Some of those evening programs were "Boston Blackie," "I was a Communist for the FBI," and "Dragnet" with Sgt. Joe Friday.

At lunchtime each day my parents would tune in to CBC to hear about the goings on of "The Gillens", out in Sunnybrae. The characters on that program became so realistic that they were thought of almost as neighbours that lived just a little further away. What I remember about that program was the theme song, "English Country Garden," and anytime I have heard that piece of music since I have been reminded of listening to that radio program.

When I was about fifteen or sixteen I received an RCA Victor record player for Christmas. It only played the small 45 RPM vinyl records, as those were new and popular at the time. To buy records I had to write to the Nieforth record store on Windmill Road in Dartmouth and they would mail me the record. Records were less than a dollar each including the shipping and postage. Some of my favorite singers were Pat Boone, Bing Crosby, Doris Day, Dean Martin, Buddy Holly and later, Bill Haley. Their songs topped the hit parade in the late 1940s and 1950s.

* * *

I loved music. We always had a piano at home. I was asked at one point, probably when I was in early elementary school, if I would take lessons. At the particular age when I was asked, there was no way I was willing to take piano lessons. It was well known that the piano teacher in the village only taught classical piano music so why would I want to do that? Later on when I was in high school, I wanted to learn to play a band instrument, but there was no opportunity to do that because our air cadet squadron did not have a band component. It has been one of my greatest regrets in later years that I never did learn to play piano, fiddle or some other musical instrument.

One winter during high school, I spent one afternoon each week going to Joan Buckler for dance lessons to learn how to waltz, foxtrot and polka. Joan was several years older than me, but she was a good dancer and I in turn learned to love to dance. Unfortunately, I was so shy that when I began to attend the school dances, I was afraid to ask a girl to dance with me. Back then, everyone sat in chairs around the walls of the school gymnasium and in order to ask someone to dance who was sitting any distance away meant being watched by everyone else still sitting. It was a mortifying experience to make a trip across the dance floor and be turned down by the girl you asked to dance. And back then only boys did the asking.

Sometimes, if too many students were glued to their chairs, the teacher chaperones would get everyone up on the floor and form the group into two large circles one within the other. The boys would be in the outer circle and the girls in the inner. The music would start and one circle would move clockwise while the other moved counter-clockwise, in opposite directions to each other. The music would then be cut off abruptly and the boy would have to dance with the closest girl in the inner circle. On one memorable occasion I ended up paired with Miss Noiles, my young, pretty, red headed French teacher. I would never have dared approach her otherwise.

After I got my driver's license, I would go to the Saturday night dances at Shirl Colburne's dance hall in the building to the west side of where Tatamagouche Brewing is located now. There would be a local three- or four-piece band made up of piano, fiddle, guitar and drums, with musicians such as Don Millard and Lloyd Tattrie. The dance music would be foxtrots, waltzes, and square sets, which might be waltz quadrilles or hop polkas. Each square set was made up of four couples, and there would be four musical selections with each set, with a caller leading the dancers in the actions for each selection of music. The actions were somewhat similar to square dancing, but the music and footwork were different.

The footwork for the polka quadrille was I believe somewhat unique to the northern part of Nova Scotia. It was locally called the Colchester County Hop. A typical musical selection by the band might be "Old MacDonald's Reel", or even an original piece composed in his head by the fiddler. Whenever paired with a partner in each of the four selections, the two dancers would match steps in a pattern which was a form of step dancing. Each action would consist of four beats: a hop and two steps, a hop and two steps, and so on. At some of the older dancehalls there were times that when every step was in sync, the dance floor would physically pulse to the beat of the music.

I developed a love for that so-called old-time dance music. Part of the fun of attending those country dances was just to hear the music. The jigs and reels really had Celtic roots, and perhaps there is something of my Scottish heritage ingrained within me. I wished I could play an instrument in one of those bands. I admire anyone who plays that type of music on the piano or fiddle, fingertips moving so naturally from memory.

Public dance admission was fifty cents, for by then prices were on the rise. During the summer there were dances at Malagash Mine, Brule Beach, and MacBain's Corner on different nights of the week. After I had my driver's license and started attending some of the dances and other youth activities, I was able to borrow the truck for transportation. Gasoline was forty to forty-two cents an Imperial gallon so by putting a dollar's worth of gas in the truck I was able to travel the countryside all evening. The odometers in vehicles back then were mechanically driven by a cable that that came up under the dash of the car. In case a father was keeping an eye on the mileage that was being racked up in an evening it was possible to reach under the dash and disconnect the odometer cable for the evening.

One of the summers that my aunt and uncle came from the States to visit the farm, they had a portable AM radio with them. Portable radios were virtually unheard of before that time. This was a vacuum tube type, battery-operated radio about the size of a man's lunch box or small cooler. Since radios in cars were not common either at that time, this portable radio was the ultimate accessory to have for an evening out on the town. Somehow, I was offered the use of the radio one evening, which I naturally accepted. Of course the radio was played nonstop, turned up loud, as I drove the streets of the village for several hours. Well, batteries did not keep going and going like the Energizer Bunny in those days so I ended up back home with a dead radio. I was not very popular with my parents when they learned the fate of the battery, as it was a unique voltage which was expensive and difficult to replace.

David MacKeen was one of my classmates in school. His father, Jimmy MacKeen, owned the Ford dealership in the village (the forerunner of Tri County Ford). When the Edsel car was introduced by Ford, one new model arrived to be for sale at MacKeen's garage. Somehow or other Dave took several of us for a drive in the Edsel one day to demonstrate how it worked. The most unique feature about the Edsel was that the gear shift was a set of pushbuttons in the centre hub of the steering wheel. The style feature that made the car look unique was the prominent chrome grill shaped like a horse collar on the front of the hood.

I also belonged to Allied Youth, which was a youth social group against alcohol. This group was sanctioned by the high school. Alcohol was not available to young people anyway as the closest liquor store was in Pictou, and even adults needed a special permit to buy it. This AY group used to hold sock hops in the school cafeteria one evening each month, chaperoned by a couple of volunteer teachers. Dancing would be to 45 or 78 rpm vinyl records. These dances were free events and popular with the high school students.

There were lots of student activities at noon hour in high school. There was a movie room where a screen and 16mm projector would be set up each day with a student operator for anyone who wished to watch a short film. There was sock hop in the music room each day that was always popular, where we could dance to the latest hit records. There would also have been a Glee Club, and there were always noon sports activities in the gym.

Back in those times, some of our more affluent relatives from away made home movies of their family's activities. Often, when they came to visit us at the farm, they would bring their stash of films and projector and take great delight in showing us all of the happenings in the lives of their family in the intervening time between visits. As I remember, watching these grainy, silent pictures became pretty tedious after the first reel or two.

* * *

I spent a lot of my spare time in my early teens along the French River, fishing, trapping and hunting. I wished that I had a boat as that would allow me to get across the water to other areas to explore. Each spring with the river breakup freshets there would be old lumber, logs and other driftwood material deposited on the intervale, coming on the flood from somewhere further upstream. One summer I was able to build a nice raft with this heavy lumber and float it in the creek that runs under the first bridge. With a long pole to push against the gravel creek bottom I was able to navigate up and down the creek.

After a summer or two navigating with my raft, I received an old secondhand wooden rowboat for my birthday. The boat had been well built but had seen better days by the time it arrived in my possession. Many hours were spent in scraping old paint, caulking the joints and repainting it inside and out. My father made a pair of oars from boards we had on hand and I bought a ship's life preserver at Tommy Pugh's war surplus store in the village.

The boat had been constructed to have an outboard motor mounted on the back. That was next on my wish list. After some negotiations with my father he agreed that we would cut some spruce logs in the Wilson Creek gully east of the farm fields. With axe and bucksaw, and the tractor to pull the downed trees up over the hillside, we managed to cut two full truckloads of logs. These were sold to the Bonnyman and Byers sawmill and I then had enough money to buy a second hand, 3 HP Evinrude outboard motor from Howard Lafrense.

I kept the boat anchored in the area of the French River where we swam. When the weather was good and the tide was right, I spent many hours on the river. I could go all the way to the village wharf by water. There were times though when the outboard motor got cantankerous and I would have to row the boat all the way back home.

Those early outboards ran on mixed gas. I think the admixture was one part of thirty-weight oil to twelve parts of regular gas. With that high ratio of oil to gas, if not mixed together exactly, it often times led to a cranky motor.

A favorite spot to swim when I was in late high school was at the village wharf. There was a public lane leading down the hill from Main Street and the wharf itself at that time was maintained by the government and was in excellent condition. It was located on the edge of the river channel so there was enough water depth even at low tide that fishing boats could tie up there. Thankfully for teenagers there was little commercial use of the wharf and someone went ahead and spiked a plank to one end of the wharf as a diving board. One season we swam first on May 22 and from then on until the last date close to the end of September.

The advantage to swimming at the wharf was that when the tide came in, the water passed over the sun-warmed sand bars of Tatamagouche Harbour, and thus was at a much warmer temperature than would have been found in some of the beaches further out the bay.

* * *

Summers on the farm at that age were fun. Dave Lombard came with his mother from Needham, Massachusetts, to spend the summer with his grandparents. Dave's parents had been born and raised in Tatamagouche, but had managed to stay in the USA once they emigrated there before the Depression. Dave's grandmothers on both the Lombard and Langille sides still lived in Tatamagouche. Dave's grandfather on his mother's side had been Ben Langille, one of the local blacksmiths. Dave would stay with his grandmother Langille at night and come to his grandmother Lombard's farm during the day. We spent most of the days together all summer, from about age ten or twelve to the end of our school years.

Summer was always the best time of year because the weather was good and I was able to be outdoors all the time. I still remember the smell of new mown hay and the air just at dusk on a warm summer evening. That, combined with the evening sound of crickets chirping, bats flitting around the barnyard catching insects, and song birds twittering as they settled for the night, created a memorable setting.

Growing up on the farm provided a veritable cornucopia for the senses. Even the smell of the dry earth of the front lawn as we lay out on a blanket in the shade of the large Manitoba Maple on a hot summer day stands out as an unforgettable experience. Waking to the sound of the roosters crowing at daybreak on sunny summer mornings. The smell of pig manure was not so pleasant, but this was minor compared to the smell of the horses pulling the sleigh on a crisp winter day. The sights and sounds of life on the farm created memories to last a lifetime.

The skies on a clear night in those early years were spectacular. Without any light sources out in the countryside, the sky would be ablaze with stars. The Milky Way was easily distinguishable and on a number of occasions we were treated to displays of Northern Lights.

There were always lots of house flies in summer and fall, drawn by the barn animals and the manure they produced, but in those times we just grabbed a fly sprayer and dosed everything with DDT. I don't remember ever being bothered by mosquitoes. That was a time when there were still songbirds everywhere and lots of bats in the evenings to feed on the insects. That was before the devastation that DDT caused to the bird population.

Hurricane Edna occurred in the year 1954. This was a really devastating storm, the first hurricane that I really remember. It was mostly a wind event in northern Nova Scotia. It caused a great deal of damage to roofs, and especially to the woodlands. Earl Lombard, on the opposite side of Lake Road from the farm, lost sheets of steel off his barn roof. These pieces of steel sheeting were blown hundreds of yards over into our hayfields. We lost three large Manitoba Maple trees that had grown for many years on our lawn. Anything that was loose around the yard was picked up by the ferocious wind and carried long distances. Parts of Maine and New Brunswick, on the west side of the storm's track, received up to eight inches of rain overnight.

I feel that winter snow storms were worse when I was young. We seemed to receive much more snow over longer periods of time. Blizzards would pile up snow drifts six to ten feet high around our barn. I have seen patches of snow remaining in sheltered areas well into the month of May.

* * *

Many families have one or another amongst their members who is viewed by the others with an ambivalent eye. In the Clark family back in those times that so-called "black sheep" was "Uncle Charlie", one of my grandfather Clark's brothers, so he would have been well into his senior years. Uncle Charlie lived in Truro, which already removed him from the local family picture. He had worked for the coal company located by the railway tracks on Pleasant Street, which I assume may have been what is now the Wilson's Fuel company. Uncle Charlie owned a small A55 Austin car, probably the forerunner of the Mini Minor, which he used on rare occasion to journey to Tatamagouche to call around to visit at various relatives.

What raised eyebrows and elicited considerable gossip was that Uncle Charlie was what was known then as a "womanizer". He had already fathered an illegitimate child in his youth, which was cause for him to be disinherited by his father Charles. One incident in my own memory was when on one of Uncle Charlie's visits he took a shine to Anne Lombard, our unmarried neighbour across the road, who was home for the summer on vacation from her nursing position in New York City. Uncle Charlie hounded Anne for about a week trying to coax her to go for a drive with him in his Austin car. Anne managed to put off his propositions until he finally gave up.

Alcohol was not a problem I was ever aware of growing up. It simply was not easily available. The closest liquor stores were in Pictou or Truro and a permit was needed to purchase and transport it. There were times, however, in the heat of the summer when my father and Earl Lombard would each order a case of beer by using Davy Bell's transfer truck to pick it up when in one of those towns for a load of freight. Now Earl's mother and my grandmother Braine were both dead set against any type of alcoholic drink, so any beer at either farm was kept very carefully hidden in the grain bins. But on especially hot days during haying season when the men were called for dinner at noon, they might be a bit slow to show up because of a quick stop in the granary for a drink of beer.

My father did not drink alcohol other than for that very occasional bottle of beer in the summertime. I do remember one time though when there was an incident that caused some consternation at the farm. On this occasion a couple of Uncle Charlie's sons had shown up early one morning from Truro to visit my father. These first cousins of his had with them that day a substantial jug of some type of moonshine, and by the time they arrived at our place they had sampled it and found it much to their liking. They thereupon convinced my father that he liked it too, and being unused to strong liquor he too was soon feeling the happy effects. Unfortunately, this was on a day when my mother was having one of her card parties with all her women friends from the community. My father, once he managed to get rid of the cousins, was forced to hide in the barn for the remainder of the day so as not to have any contact with the bridge ladies.

* * *

My father was always very innovative. He probably would have been a very good engineer. Whenever something needed to be fixed or something needed to be built from scratch, he was always able to come up with a way to plan and do the task without much financial cost. One example was a wooden snow plow for the front of the tractor. This was attached to the undercarriage of the tractor and could be adjusted to the height of the road surface by chains and clevises attached to the front axle. A scrap road grader wear bar scrounged from the highway department kept the bottom of the plow from wearing out on the gravelled lane. He created a cab for the tractor using a wood frame with canvas covering and an old picture frame and glass for the windshield. To give the tractor more traction in snow he added a wooden platform to the drawbar at the back that would hold several bags of grain to add weight to the rear end.

There was one season when we had an infestation of rats in the pig shed. The shed was attached to the end of the barn and these rats nested in the hay mow of the barn and had holes through the wall to access feed in the pig's trough at night. My father's solution to the problem was to seal up the interior of the pig pen by nailing sheet metal to the tops of the pen walls, and sealing all the rat access holes but one. He built a trap door over that one hole that was held open by a trip cord leading outdoors. The pigs were moved to another pen, but he continued to put out feed in the pig trough. The rats soon became used to this new environment and several nights later Dad was ready to spring his trap. We sneaked quietly into position to pull the trip cord on the trap door. The trap door worked as planned so that when we turned on the light over the pig pen the scene was a horde of frantic rats wildly trying to get out of the pen. The sheet metal also worked well, preventing the scampering rats from climbing up out of the pen.

Perhaps not for the weak of heart, but we did not have rat phobias. We climbed into the pen in our rubber boots, and proceeded to kill the rats with shovels. We killed twenty-six rats that one night and did not see another rat around the barn for a number of years afterward.

* * *

At some point in the early 1950s I bought my own rifle for target practice. It was a .22 calibre repeater that I purchased through mail order from the Eaton's catalogue. I built my own sand-filled target out behind the barn and sharpened my marksmanship skills. Besides the rats in the barn, I also used the rifle for hunting ducks and partridge, and I ranged over an area of a mile or so in radius from home. After I was old enough to have an adult hunting license I purchased another rifle to hunt deer. This was a 30-30 Winchester, lever action rifle, which I bought at the Forbes Bros General Store in Denmark.

Up behind the village, back of the farms along the Lake Road and across country to the Cooper Road, was a large tract of forest land, perhaps three or four hundred acres. I used to hunt in those woods, sometimes with my cousin Alec Norman, when he was home for a weekend.

There was an old settlers' road through these woods from the Lake Road leading in the direction of the Cooper's Bridge, called the Four Pound Road. This road got its name as a result of a government grant in early times allotting four Pounds Sterling towards its construction. This road ran south from a point about a hundred metres west of the present power company substation on the Lake Road. Only a wide row of trees remains now at the Lake Road end, but seventy some years ago this was a well travelled wood road for use of the woodlot owners.

Another old settler's era road ran along the boundary between the Lombard and Alvah MacKinnon farms, parallel to the Lake Road and approximately a quarter mile south. This road had almost disappeared, except that it was still able to be traced where it went down over the riverbank to the upper end of the French River interval at a point where the river could have been forded at the head of tide. This may have been part of the early Acadian transportation route leading along the French River and over the mountain to the Acadian settlement on the Bay of Fundy side at Chiganois.

I loved the woods and sometimes after school I would take an axe and go over to the riverbank and chop trees to clear a little park like area. At one point I had about an acre of nice wooded parkland in the level area along the top of the riverbank behind the west fields. This area would still make a nice site for a cabin or a house, with a beautiful view up the French River valley.

* * *

In high school I joined Royal Canadian Air Cadets, which was then a school activity for a couple of periods one afternoon a week. In cadets, I was a member of the marksmanship team and I was the best shot in the squadron. The rifle range was up between the roof trusses above the classroom ceilings of the school. We used old 303 calibre Lee Enfield army rifles that had been re-bored to shoot 22 calibre bullets. I won a Lord Strathcona gold award for highest score at a provincial cadet marksmanship competition in Halifax.

One of our squadron's program activities of course was to learn about airplanes and flying. On one sunny Saturday when I was in Grade 10 we travelled by school bus to Debert, to the airport located on the old military base. There we boarded a twin engine, propeller driven, C-47 Dakota aircraft that had been sent from RCAF Greenwood to provide us with the flight experience. The flight took us up over Tatamagouche, and each of us in turn got to take a look into the cockpit to see the pilots and the instrumentation. The Dakota was the workhorse aircraft of the war years and was one of the most significant transport aircraft ever produced. It had a cruising speed of 200 miles per hour and held from 20 to 30 passengers. Back then each of us had a parachute in case of emergency. This was my first experience in an airplane.

Two different summers in high school I attended the two-week summer air cadet camps at RCAF Greenwood. These were good experiences. The food was plentiful and good, with lots of variety. It was a bit of a revelation to me to see platter after platter piled high with food in the cafeteria as we lined up for our meals. I met a lot of guys from Brookfield and other parts of the Maritimes. Again I had perfect scores in marksmanship on the rifle range. The only downside of that camp was being bussed out to Lake George once each week to swim, and being forced into the cold water (which was the officers' means of making us all have a bath).

Everyone had to make their own cot in the morning, which had to be perfect for daily inspection. There was also a drill parade each morning before we went off in our squads to our designated activity for the morning. An old wartime Lancaster Bomber was still stationed at Greenwood at that time so we got to board that plane and see all of its inner workings.

In high school, my aim was to become a pilot in the RCAF. That ended up being ruled out when it was learned that I was slightly red/green colour blind.

While I was in high school, I also joined the RCAF Ground Observer Corps. This would have been at the beginning of the cold war. We were tasked with keeping our eyes on the skies for signs of strange aircraft that might be spying on Canada, or for the beginning of an enemy invasion. I participated in several test exercises where we manned a watchtower built on top of the Tatamagouche Royal Canadian Legion building, and we were required to telephone in to headquarters and report the description of any airplane that happened to fly over us.

* * *

At some point in my early teens. someone bought a woodlot next to ours on the Slade Road. Since the boundary lines had become undefined over the passage of time the new owner decided to have his land surveyed. He hired Howard Murray, PLS, from Earltown, to do the survey. Back then, when a land survey was being done, it was common practice for adjoining property owners to be on site to ensure everyone was in agreement with the re-established boundary. My father and I accompanied Howard and the new adjoining owner to cut out and blaze the boundary line. Howard used an old surveyor's staff compass and a sixty-six foot Günter's link chain to measure up the angles and distances. I was on one end of the chain to measure the distances. That was my first experience with land surveying.

* * *

Television did not become available until I was in high school. The first television in the area was a huge cabinet model in the window of the Forbes Bros Furniture Store in Denmark. The set was left turned on most of the time, but only once in a long while when the atmospheric conditions made the signal skip, would there be a snowy picture from a broadcast station in Boston. Eventually though, the CBC began broadcasting from Halifax and Charlottetown. The picture from Halifax was often "too snowy" to see well.

I believe that programming in those early days was limited mostly to the evening hours. From the time of sign-off at midnight to sign-on the following day, the TV station broadcast a "test pattern" which one could use to adjust the quality of the TV picture. And in the first years the picture was black and white. Colour was to come later.

When we finally got a TV set of our own, we received CBC programs from Charlottetown, PEI, because it was only fifteen miles away, directly across the Northumberland Strait. With a big aluminum aerial on the roof of the house we could receive that one TV channel. Then we were able to watch the Don Messer Show, Singalong Jubilee, and the Ed Sullivan Show on Saturday and Sunday nights.

One song from the Don Messer show was particularity memorable. The show would always close with Charlie Chamberlin and Marg Osborne singing "Till We Meet Again". That song started off with the words "Smile the while you kiss me sad adieu," and ended with "Till we meet again."

My father rigged up the roof aerial on top of a long metal post that went from ground level up the side of the house to several feet above the peak of the roof. The post had a lever at ground level so that by going outdoors it was possible to turn the post and aerial so it pointed in the direction of Halifax and thereby we could sometimes pick up a second TV station if the weather was right.

* * *

While I was growing up, gambling was considered a sin by my parents, my grandmother, and our neighbour Mrs. Nellie Lombard. This was never really a problem as I was not exposed to any form of gambling that I was aware of. Then there was an incident late one summer while Dave Lombard was still visiting with his grandparents. One of Dave's uncles was Bill Langille, who operated Langille's Meat Market in the village. Perhaps we were old enough by then that Dave was working for Bill part time in the market. Now Bill followed the horse races in Truro. On one occasion, probably during

Exhibition week in Truro, Bill invited Dave Lombard and me to go with him to the horse races. This was a new experience for me and it was for the most part boring, standing around for long periods waiting for a race that only lasted a couple of minutes. In consultation with Bill, however, we studied the race card for the individual times of the various horses in previous races, and Dave and I decided to wager on one of the races. We split the price, a dollar each on a two-dollar ticket. When the race was over the ticket actually paid out four dollars, so we each gained an illicit dollar that evening. That was the first and only time I have ever gambled on a horse race, but I am able to say that I have never lost money gambling on the horses.

* * *

I obtained my driver's license as soon as I turned sixteen. I did not take a driver's test. Davy Bell, our neighbour, was the examiner and he just signed the form and told me I was good to go. He knew I had been driving the tractor for years.

My grandmother Braine came to live with us after the death of my grandfather. He had died suddenly of a heart attack in Glen Margaret, on his way to make a medical house call. My grandmother had a 1955 Chevrolet Bel Air car and she liked to go for a drive every day. After I had my driver's license, I was drafted to be her chauffeur for these short drives; usually just to the village, but sometimes exploring back country roads.

The '55 Chev was an excellent car. Built by General Motors and completely redesigned that year from previous years, it got up to twenty-five miles per gallon with a six-cylinder engine. This was the beginning of a decade of radical style changes by the five major automobile manufacturing companies. Those companies were Ford, General Motors, Chrysler, American Motors (Hudson/Nash) and Studebaker/Packard. The different General Motors' series cars were Chevrolet, Pontiac, Buick, Oldsmobile, and Cadillac. Each of those brands came in different models. The Ford series were Ford, Monarch, Mercury and Lincoln.

It seemed during the 1950s that most young males of my generation were obsessed with cars. Most of us could identify the make, model and year of every car on the road. Of course, we each had our own opinions of which car company was the best and of the model we dreamed to purchase if we were ever to have enough money.

There were many differences in these older cars, more even than with the cars of the late sixties. Cars in the late forties and fifties did not have signal lights; the driver had to hold his arm out the window to warn of a planned turn by bending the arm at the elbow and pointing either up or down to signal a right or left turn. The front seat was bench style and customized seat covers were an extra. The car starter was a knob on the floor to be pushed with one's foot once the ignition key was turned on. Cars had standard shift transmissions. Air conditioning back then was an air scoop on the hood, just in front of the windshield, which was opened by pushing forward a lever located under the dash. The windows of the two front doors were divided so that the front triangular section could be pushed outward to also act as a scoop to divert outside air into the car's interior. White wall tires were the rage to fancy up the exterior look of the vehicle. The whitewalls could be bought separately from the tires and installed against the plain black tire as the tire was being mounted on its steel rim. Other fads those days were fender skirts, curb feelers and colouring the parking lights amber with the addition of shellac. This was a time of course long before the advent of seat belts.

For those of us lucky enough to have the use of a car and money for gas, the evening could be spent cruising back and forth along Main Street of the village, showing off the car and keeping an eye out for girls.

* * *

I eventually went to Dr. Ralph Langille, a rough talking, ex-army dentist practicing in Truro, to get fillings in most of my back teeth. Dr. Langille's solution to my buck tooth problem was to tell me to go to a medical doctor to get my front teeth pulled, and he would then make up dental plate to replace them. I went back to Tatamagouche and dropped in to Dr. Austin Creighton's office without an appointment. Dr. Creighton was a medical GP and by then had replaced Dr. Dan Murray as our family doctor. I told Dr. Creighton of my recommendation from Dr. Langille and he promptly froze my jaw and yanked out my four upper front teeth.

He charged me three dollars for his fee that day. This was before Medicare, when doctors still charged for their services.

After my mouth healed, I went back to Dr. Langille and he made up a denture for me for thirty-five dollars.

* * *

On one of the drives with my grandmother she asked me if I would like to become a medical doctor and she offered to pay my way through university. Without serious thought I said no. At that stage in my life I had my heart set on becoming a pilot, and did not even consider medicine as a career choice. I have often wondered since about what would have happened if I had agreed? Unfortunately, I was not mature enough then to appreciate that opportunity. My grandfather, two of my great uncles, a great aunt and a first cousin had all been GP doctors. My sister, four aunts and two nephews were nurses. I guess the genes lean in that direction on both sides of the family.

More and more in recent years I have come to regret that I did not give greater consideration to going into medicine.

CHAPTER 10 - A SPECIAL CHRISTMAS MEMORY

All of us have mental images of special events or happenings going back to our earliest childhood. My vivid Christmas morning memory goes back to the year I received my teddy bear. I would have been three or four years old, so not only is it one of my first Christmas Day memories, it has been one of my most lasting.

The image still so clear from that long-ago day is of me coming down the narrow stairway into the farmhouse kitchen early Christmas morning and shyly staring at the spot near the kitchen woodstove where my stocking had been carefully hung on a nail the previous evening. I know my parents and older sister were also present, but they are only shadows on the fringes of my mental picture. Certainly my father would have been up earlier to build a fire in the woodstove, which now radiated its heat to make the kitchen cozy and inviting.

But none of these things registered. Santa Claus had come. My eyes were locked only on what poked from the top of that old beige cotton stocking. All I could see was a white face with black ears and glassy eyes that reflected a yellow beam of light from the kerosene lamp on the kitchen table.

How long I stood in wide-eyed wonder I do not know. Someone must have broken the spell and urged me to go see what was in the stocking, because I know my next act was to remove the small black and white teddy bear from its stocking cocoon to examine it and hold its soft fur to my face.

Set aside without further thought was the stocking, still with its undiscovered pieces of red, white and green ribbon candy, an assortment of unshelled nuts, and an orange in the toe. I am sure my parents must have been a bit let down when I was less than excited about the orange. To them this would have been a special treat, unavailable other than at Christmastime during the early 1940's war years.

It was understood of course that Santa had filled the stocking and brought this special gift. Being so young I had no comprehension that living on a small farm in those war years meant there was no money for anything but the barest essentials. Only in later years did I come to realize where the teddy bear came from.

My grandparents had come to visit for Christmas that year from Annapolis Royal. The visit itself was a unique event, as travel at that time of year with gas rationing and unpredictable weather was not reasonable. They had come by train. Yes, it was possible to go from Annapolis Royal to Tatamagouche by train in those days.

* * *

My grandfather was a medical doctor in the days before Medicare, so there was little extra money there either. Payment for delivering a baby might be a bag of potatoes, or a haunch of deer meat, but there must have been a bit of extra cash set aside by a frugal grandmother. Enough to splurge to make a grandson's Christmas a special time.

Christmas Day was a time of religious celebration and all of it would have happened at home. If there had been a church service, I doubt we would have attended. That would have required my father to have hitched up Belle and Molly (our team of horses) to the bobsled, and all of us bundling up in winter clothing for the two mile trip to the village, with a couple of Buffalo robes to keep out the cold. My grandmother was a deeply religious woman, so if unable to attend church, I am sure she would have read to us the Christmas story from her King James Bible.

Christmas Day would have been spent quietly, between the kitchen and the parlor. The day would have been like a Sunday where the only work performed would have been the essential tasks of feeding and milking the cows, and on this day, the necessary preparations in the kitchen to cook Christmas dinner.

The parlor, which would have been closed off and unheated in the winter, was opened up for the few days of my grandparent's visit. A spruce tree would have been cut and brought in from the back pasture on Christmas Eve Day and decorated in one corner of the room on Christmas Eve. The tree would have been draped with tinsel icicles, red and green glass balls, white paper-mâché bells trimmed with silver glitter, and a rope garland of coloured glass beads. There were no strings of lights because this would have been at a time before we had electricity at the farm.

After the morning chores in the barn were finished and everyone had eaten a breakfast of oatmeal porridge with thick fresh cream and maple syrup, we would all have gathered in the parlor to open gifts that had magically appeared under the tree. Gifts were always practical things that the recipient needed anyway. My sister and I would get new hand knit mittens or wool socks. My father and grandfather would get socks or a new tie or handkerchief, and my mother and grandmother perhaps a box of Moirs "Pot of Gold" chocolates.

When the few gifts had been opened and everything tidied up, my father and grandfather would sit in the kitchen or parlor and smoke their pipes and discuss the latest war news from overseas.

The women meanwhile would be busy with kitchen chores and preparations for Christmas dinner. The menu for dinner would consist of mashed potatoes, mashed turnip, squash, carrots or parsnips. All of these vegetables would have been grown in the garden and stored in the unheated, mud-floor cellar during the winter. A rooster, raised in the previous months and killed a couple of days before Christmas, would be roasted in the oven of the woodstove. All of the cooking would have taken place on the Enterprise wood stove standing prominently on one side of the kitchen. The heat would be regulated by my mother's adjustments to the damper and her selective choice of pieces of hard and soft wood to fuel the stove.

Christmas dinner would have been eaten at the dining room table, the dining room having been opened up and heated just for this occasion. The table would have been set with a white lace tablecloth and for this special meal, the good dishes and silver would have brought out of storage from the heirloom mahogany sideboard. The white dishes with gold trim and the set of "Tipped" pattern silverware had come down through the generations from my great grandmother. The sideboard was a prized possession of my mother, an antique even then, having also come down through several generations of the Braine family.

The meal would begin with grace said by my grandfather, during which we all had to bow our heads and close our eyes. Then the food would be served with ceramic platters being passed so everyone could load their plates. There would not have been any wine as my grandmother was dead set against any type of alcoholic beverage. The adults would have had tea, and my sister and I would have had glasses of fresh milk, perhaps still warm from the cows that morning. There would have been little candy dishes at each place setting with nuts and a couple of pieces of homemade fudge in each. The fudge too would be a special treat because sugar was rationed during the war. Dessert would have been squash or mincemeat pie. There would also have been fancy plates with pieces of white or dark fruitcake and shortbread cookies.

Everyone would have had lots to eat. My father would have gone down to the cellar every few hours to throw another log in the wood furnace so the house would be warm and cozy. After any leftover food was put away in the cold storage box and the dishes were hand washed, the women would have a bit of time to relax, perhaps with a favorite book or a needlework activity. The men would smoke and perhaps doze in a rocking chair or on the kitchen couch.

My time, of course, would have been spent playing with my new teddy bear.

CHAPTER 11 - BETTER TIMES

There was never any doubt growing up that I did not want to stay on the farm as a career. Even though huge changes were beginning to take place in agriculture and farm management, the financial outlook for farmers when I graduated from high school was bleak, and from the perspective of my experience the lifestyle was unappealing.

I was not alone. I don't think any of my schoolmates had aspirations to be farmers. Many of my classmates struck out for Southern Ontario where the economy was booming and there were all kinds of employment opportunities. This out-migration of young people from Nova Scotia to Ontario was similar to the movement of my father's generation to Massachusetts and the present generation to Alberta. Several of my schoolmates eventually ended up with Tim Horton's franchises through Tatamagouche connections to the Ron Joyce and Archie Jollymore families.

At that time, there were more than 100,000 small farms in Nova Scotia. But this was a time of huge change with the beginning of the demise of small family farms in Nova Scotia.

The year I graduated from high school I got a summer job as a grocery clerk at the Bonnyman and Bell general store in Tatamagouche. The hours were long. On Monday, Thursday and Friday, I worked from 8AM to 6PM with an hour off for lunch. On Tuesday and Saturday, I worked from 8AM to 10PM with an hour for lunch and an hour for supper. On Wednesday and Sunday, the store was closed. I was paid twenty-four dollars a week for a 51-hour work week.

Harry Bonnyman had a little cubbyhole out behind the section of general merchandise which he used as a part time office. At the end of my work shift on Saturday night, I went back to see Harry and he counted out my twenty-four dollars in cash and handed it over to me. A week or so later I splurged three dollars of my pay for a pair of slim blue jeans I had been eyeing on the clothing shelf along the west wall of the store.

On another occasion I purchased a single plug of chewing tobacco. I did not smoke, but was curious about the effect of chewing. Later on, back at home I slipped over to the wooded hillside out of sight, cut off a bite sized piece of the tobacco plug with my jackknife, and popped in into my mouth. It seemed like only minutes chewing on this cud of the stuff when the unanticipated effects hit. One thing led to another where I was first dizzy, then sick to my stomach. As soon as the worst was over, I buried the remainder of the plug in the woods and that ended any further curiosity to chew tobacco.

The store owners, Davy Bell and Harry Bonnyman, and Jack Coulter the meat cutter, had the prices of all the grocery items in their heads. There were no prices marked on any of the grocery shelves. The cash register did not have a mechanical adding machine component. When customers came to the counter with their basket of items it was up to me to list each item on a cash receipt book along with the price, and add up the total myself. That was great training to quickly add numbers in my head. My greatest difficulty with that job was memorizing the price of every item on the shelves and the cost per pound for items that were bought in bulk.

Many foodstuffs were sold in bulk. Customers would bring their own containers or jugs to the store for molasses, vinegar, kerosene, etc. Molasses came to the store in a huge wooden puncheon or oversize barrel. The bung would be removed and a tap inserted, then the barrel would be tipped onto its side on a stand and jugs could be filled by turning the tap or spigot. Kerosene for lamps was handled by similar means. Sugar and other dry bulk materials were sold by weight, in pounds and ounces, usually scooped out of wooden bins into paper bags and then weighed and priced at the counter. Cheddar cheese came in a heavy cylindrical block, about a foot and a half in diameter and four inches high. It sat on the end of a hardwood counter with a semicircular glass cover. The cheese was bought by the customer cutting the desired sized wedge out of the block with a large knife, then bringing it to the cash register to be weighed and wrapped. Meat was cut right from the animal carcass and weighed and wrapped in waxed brown paper at the meat counter.

Many people at that time bought their groceries on credit with the store. The cash receipt book had carbon copies. The customer would receive one copy, and the original would be filed away with the customer's name in a storage rack for that purpose behind the counter. When customers had money available, they would come in and make a payment on their credit line with the store. Credit cards were still in the future.

My work stint clerking in the grocery store did have one positive outcome. I determined that besides farming, clerking in a store or some other manual labour type of job was not going to be a lifelong career for me. There had to be a more appealing future waiting out there somewhere.

* * *

After I found out that my colour blindness would not permit me to become a pilot my next career choice was to be a forester. I did not know exactly what a forester did, but I had always loved being out in the woods. I applied to University of New Brunswick in Fredericton and was accepted into the Forestry Baccalaureate program. I was really impressed with the UNB university jackets, which were red with black letters, the university colours. As I was getting ready to register at UNB, I learned there was a huge demand for engineers, and it seemed there were better job opportunities in that profession.

It was suggested I should switch to Electrical Engineering instead, which I did.

That turned out to be a huge mistake. New Brunswick in those days had Grade 13 in high school. It was deemed to be equivalent to the first year of a University program. My Grade 12 or Senior Matriculation in Nova Scotia was considered to be equivalent to Grade 13 in NB and thus to first year of University. So with my Nova Scotia Grade 12, I was accepted into the second year of the Engineering program at UNB. However, I had not taken the Analytical Geometry component of Mathematics that the New Brunswick students had. Without this prerequisite to Calculus I was unable to catch up as we jumped right into Calculus 230.

University was a good learning experience even if some of my courses did not go so well. One of my courses was in land surveying, which I did enjoy. Engineering students at that time required a language credit so I enrolled in an extra course, first in German, which did not go well, so I switched to French. Still no oral French, but my background high school grammar courses did manage to gain me my language credit. I participated in several student activities, attended arts concerts and university sports games. I was independent and exposed to a completely new cultural experience. I boarded with former friends of my parents who were originally from Tatamagouche, so I did not experience life in residence. This was another mistake. I did not meet other students except in class, and thus did not make any lasting friends.

Lord Beaverbrook was a patron of the university. When he visited, he drove through the campus in his chauffeured black Rolls Royce limousine. The Hon. John Diefenbaker also visited one time, and I happened to be in a hallway as he walked through. Ever the politician, the Dief turned to me and stuck out his hand. That is how I got to shake hands with the Prime Minister of Canada.

At some point in my early years, my parents had taken out a one thousand dollar life insurance policy for me from Jim Langille, who sold insurance in the village for Great West Life. They must have scrimped in the lean times to find the money for the payments. The policy was one that built up savings, so when I went off to university I was able to cash it in and it was enough to cover all my expenses for my year. Full tuition, room and board, text books, supplies, travel, and spending money all came in under my thousand dollar budget for that year.

After that year of university engineering, I worked for 14 months on a survey crew with the Gatineau Power Company, to carry out the preliminary route survey for a new high voltage transmission line in the Paugan Falls to St. Agathe region of the province of Quebec. Our work was directed from the company head office in Hull. During the work week, we travelled from Hull to the different fieldwork areas in Volkswagen crew vans. I shared an apartment in Ottawa on weekends with a group of fellow university students who also worked for Gatineau Power, and for the federal government.

Those were fun times. I finally had a steady income, my weekly work expenses were covered by my employer, and best of all I now had a group of friends. Living in the city of Ottawa after growing up in the village of Tatamagouche was quite a revelation. Many of my crew members and apartment mates had other connections in Ottawa, so our circle of friends expanded. We had an enjoyable social life when we were all together on the weekends. The city of Hull, Quebec, just on the opposite side of the river from Ottawa, had a much more open-minded nightlife than the Province of Ontario in those days. There were night clubs in Hull that brought in big name entertainers such as Louis Armstrong, Tony Bennet, Connie Frances, and other top entertainers of that era. I would only have seen these artists on the Ed Sullivan Show otherwise.

Ottawa was a city that had an overabundance of single females because of the civil service centered there. Both the Ottawa Civic Hospital and the federal civil service had residences for single women. We soon made our acquaintance known to some of the Ottawa Civic student nurses by phoning the residence and saying we were Maritime university students, new to the city, and asking if there might be anyone who was free for a date on that particular evening. We made quite a number of female friends that way.

At the apartment I learned to play Bridge and our group of friends spent many weekend daytime hours playing cards. After I had saved enough money, I was able to buy a second hand 1953 Meteor car (the Canadian version of the Ford model), for $535. I was then able to broaden my horizons even more. That was the car I drove home when I returned to Nova Scotia.

At the end of the second summer in Ottawa I came back to Nova Scotia and enrolled in the two-year land surveying course at the Nova Scotia Land Survey Institute (now COGS/NSCC) in Lawrencetown, Annapolis County.

CHAPTER 12 - PARTING THOUGHTS

In concluding this series of recollections, I feel I have described a much different way of life back in the 1940s and 1950s from that which we live today. Whether the differences are positive or negative depends on one's perspective. Looking back, I am sure there were life lessons learned growing up that I would not have learned otherwise. But also looking back, I wish the level of knowledge and understanding of the outside world had been greater. Narrow-mindedness occurred in those times because people did not know any better than what their parents and grandparents had instilled in them as being the way things had been for generations. Changes to an ingrained mindset did not evolve easily.

I was born during times of financial and physical hardship for many people. Growing up, it was instilled in me to be extremely cautious in my outlook and to always give serious consideration before taking chances on any financial investments, job choices or other life altering changes. I feel that this same philosophy held back many

Nova Scotians from taking charge of their lives and being unafraid to invest in their future.

Back then it was not even a consideration of my parents to borrow money to make improvements to the farm or to make any major expenditures. If a significant purchase was planned, then money was saved carefully until there was enough cash on hand to pay for it.

I hesitate to offer any guidance to those who have read this so far. My only suggestion would be to consider wisely any advice you are given before acting on it. Some of the advice I received when I was growing up turned out not to be helpful. For example, my father told me on several occasions that it was foolish to invest in land because it was not worth anything. Land is now worth hundreds of times what it was back then. My father, also because of what happened to the stock market at the beginning of the Great Depression was dead set against any investment in the stock market. Yet the stock market, despite its fluctuations, has always recovered its losses and continues to grow.

Thus, when it came time for their retirement years, my parents did not have any investments, savings or retirement plans. If it had not been for the Old Age Pension and the Supplement they would have been in dire straits.

I would exhort the reader to always be conscious of how he or she would like to live in the future. It is especially important nowadays to have a solid financial plan for your later years. Retirement may seem to be in the far distant future when you are young, but the years pass quickly and it is wise to make long range plans early. Many retirement pensions at this time are underfunded, fewer young people are contributing, low interest rates mean the plans do not increase the way they once did, and pensioners are now living longer and using up the funds that are there. Many corporate and government pension plans are approaching a breaking point right now. People who have opted for early retirement may eventually face a devastating future. I strongly advise investing in an RRSP or other solid savings plan as early in life as possible. The difference between putting money in an RRSP very early in life and waiting even a decade or so is astounding. It might mean the difference between an enjoyable retirement lifestyle or being a ward of the state.

* * *

Significant societal changes took place in the 1960s. It was the beginning of a time of prosperity and increased expectations. It was also a time of awakening, of becoming aware of new truths, and learning that some of the common beliefs held so implicitly by previous generations were not as absolute as we had always been taught to believe. Fact-based science began to replace blind faith. Perhaps this was not so obvious to me at the time as being more than just the evolution of my life after graduating from high school and leaving my home environment. But it was a time when technology began to blossom, rates of pay began to increase annually, and attitudes toward others of different race, colour or religion very slowly began to improve.

It is hard to believe the changes that have occurred over my lifetime. So many modern conveniences have been developed that we now take for granted. As only one small example, ball point pens appeared as "liquid pencils" when I was in about Grade five or six. Before that we did schoolwork with lead pencils and wrote up projects and exams with fountain pens. A bottle of ink and a blotter were necessary school supplies. So much of our modern technology could not even have been envisioned while I was still in school.

At a land surveyor's conference in the early 1960s someone predicted that the big desktop, crank operated adding machines would someday be the size of a package of cigarettes. Many laughed, thinking this was a joke. But as it has turned out, so much of the science fiction of those times is now reality.

It is mind blowing to consider how knowledge has increased and information is now able to be transmitted across the world in the blink of an eye. Encyclopedia salesmen, once a common career choice, went the way of the dinosaurs.

I have experienced almost unbelievable changes in technology in my lifetime. My first surveying experience was with a magnetic compass and sixty-six foot link chain, using equipment and methods virtually unchanged in the previous two hundred years, but present day land surveyors use Global Positioning System technology to determine the position of points on the ground to millimetre accuracy. I drew land plans by hand with India ink on tracing linen, yet now it is standard to have all the information downloaded into a computer and then fed to a laser printer that effortlessly pumps out a beautifully detailed property map. This was beyond the realm of my imagination back when I was commissioned as a professional land surveyor.

I feel that I have been extremely fortunate to live through this time period, these decades following the war years. This has been generally an unprecedented time of peace, innovation and prosperity, with huge advances in people's state of health and in generally more tolerant social attitudes. It has been a time unequalled in human development.

It has been a time especially in this local part of the world when people felt safe in their homes and on the streets. This area of Nova Scotia has been home to a gentle lifestyle removed from most the conflicts that plague many parts of the world.

But perhaps we have become far too complacent. Life has been a little bit too easy for some of the current generation. With higher wages and easy access to credit, too many people have little concern for what may happen in the future.

I am becoming increasingly pessimistic about what the future will bring. Political forces and racial tensions are fermenting in other countries (especially in the United States) which do not bode well. I see civil unrest happening in the United States that could boil over and initiate a level of chaos across the rest of the world. There are many similarities to what was happening in Germany in the 1930s. A large segment of the American population has been brainwashed by a tyrant President, a tabloid media and radical right-wing talk show hosts. Much of the American media no longer reports factual news, but instead slants its coverage of events depending on the political influence of its individual policy making powers that be. Huge segments of the population only tune in to one end of the spectrum or the other, and become so set in their opinions that they refuse to listen or even tolerate anyone else's views on any particular issue. One major media network blatantly spews out exaggerations, political propaganda, conspiracy theories and outright lies that only serve to solidify the idiocy of an already brainwashed political "base."

Americans are notoriously ill-informed on events happening outside their own country. Here again, the media is partly at fault in sensationalizing the patriotism of its news coverage within the country and ignoring the contributions that other countries make to life on this planet. There is a whole world outside the US borders, but the average American is probably unaware of how people in other countries live. Most Americans are blissfully oblivious to how their politics and their paranoia are viewed by the rest of the world. They have no concept of the loss of respect that has occurred for their once great American democracy. Their President (at the time of writing this in 2019) is viewed as a laughingstock by other world leaders.

Here in Canada, and in other countries as well, we are inundated with media coverage of American politics. We shudder at what is happening to a once great neighboring country. With a leader who is a buffoon, braggart, bully, narcissist, xenophobe, liar, cheat, misogynist, adulterer, etc. it is hard to understand why he is so admired by "his base" of evangelical Christians.

The United States of America during the last half of the twentieth century was always looked up to by the rest of the world as the leading democracy worldwide and greatly admired for the freedoms of its people. That observation is changing rapidly with the irrational actions of the President and an estranged Congress. The current leadership can be likened to that of a third world country. America in 2019 has fallen to number twenty-one in the ranking of democratic countries around the world, just barely ahead of Costa Rica.

Shame on the segment of the US population that blindly believes the misinformation being fed to it. Conditions in some parts of America approach those of a fascist regime. Those who ignore history are doomed to repeat it.

I predict that China will become the dominant world power in the near future. The military and economic aspirations of China's leadership will ensure that the country expands its influence into Africa, Latin America and the Middle East. Political instability in America and Europe will provide an open season for Chinese influence in these regions. I feel it would be wise for the younger generation of today to be studying Mandarin as a second language.

I hope the time never comes when some catastrophic event forces us to go back again to survival living as took place back in the time between the Great Depression and the end of the Second World War. Only with excellent general knowledge, a determined mindset, a strong survival instinct and common-sense preparation would it be possible to adapt to a much simpler way of life. It would be wise to always keep in mind what the future may hold in store.

When the idea first came to me to do this write up, it was my intention only to jot down some tidbits of old knowledge on how to live simply off the land if the reader were ever to go back to live on the farm at Tatamagouche. It seems, however that I have gotten carried away and have added some family history and my reminiscences of various aspects of life in the 1940s and 1950s. I have described to the best of my knowledge my own memories of growing up during a time when there was a war raging across the world. Those were difficult times for most people living through that time period. I have also included some family and local history to add a bit of perspective to life in those times.

Tatamagouche played an important role in the past history of Nova Scotia; the knowledge of which I fear is quickly becoming lost to most people. I hope that something causes that to change. Perhaps someone who reads the foregoing may be intrigued enough to delve further. I believe there are opportunities to promote the historical significance of the area, both for local general knowledge and perhaps as a draw for historical tourism. How many people nowadays know of the number of majestic sailing ships built along the Tatamagouche waterfront, or of the location of the Acadian village that was the first site for the expulsion of these settlers from the province? How many know of the existence of Fort Franklin, or of the British vs French and Mi'kmaq naval battle that took place in Tatamagouche Bay?

* * *

Much of the information and the time frames for the happenings I have described in the foregoing are a product of family anecdotes and diaries, my memories of experiences of that period of time, and historical information published by individuals knowledgeable about events that happened in earlier times. Any opinions expressed are my own.

I am fortunate in many ways to have had the experiences I did while growing up and I hope that anyone who reads this will also give some serious thought to how we live nowadays in comparison.

Readers are reminded that the 1940s and 1950s were very different times with very different cultural norms, so if certain attitudes are seen in a different light than we would view them today, we should just be thankful that some things have changed for the better. It is wise that we learn about the attitudes of those times, but we should also be aware that the past is past and we need to concentrate our efforts on continuing to improve our outlook toward others in the future.

It is my hope that my memory has served me well, but I ask that I be forgiven if a few discrepancies show up in the timing of any of the events mentioned.

Dave Clark, December 2019

POSTSCRIPT

It has now been months since this narrative was released in print format on Amazon, and several years since I began the first draft. Our lives have been altered in even the relatively short time since the second edition of the book was edited and published by my son Jonathan. Lifestyle changes have taken place that were first alluded to in my stated purpose for writing the narrative, but certainly I never envisioned what has happened due to the worldwide spread of the Covid-19 virus. Society has evolved quickly as a result, and I fear that even more change is still in store for us.

Sections of the economy have been devastated as a result of health and safety mandates implemented to reduce the spread of the virus. Businesses have been forced to close, and multitudes of people have lost their jobs and thus their sources of livelihood. For others, the workplace has changed irrevocably. Those who can work online are able to work virtually anywhere in the world where there is internet access. Many can now work from their home environment. However, those in the tourism and service industries will be impacted for years to come.

The healthy booming economy that we knew just a year ago will not recover in the foreseeable future. In the meantime, there will be a period of inflation and recession, perhaps even a deep depression. National governments are simply printing paper money to try to keep society on course, and will build up huge national debts that can never be paid off.

As I write during these last few works, I have just watched the national conventions of the two American political parties. It is difficult to choose the appropriate words to describe the political turmoil that has overtaken what was once a leading democracy in the world. To watch the propaganda emanating from the current President, and from his family and hangers on, is sickening. The misleading statements and outright lies are only intended to invigorate the President's base of voters, and to stoke his own overinflated ego. But for those close-minded Americans already brainwashed by watching only the radical right-wing commentators of Fox News, nothing will open their minds to any other point of view.

It is scary that the two political parties hold such extreme points of view in opposition to each other. One party is comprised of both the very well-to-do who support the Administration because of the financial perks they have received, and of the blue-collar evangelicals who believe in the President because of his promises to fix all of their perceived evils. The other party also has its share of rabble rousers, who have taken some good platforms to the extreme left. Proposed improvements to social programs to help the indigent are denigrated by the Administration as conspiracies to create a socialist state.

As the rest of the world views what is happening within the political system of the United States, we have to wonder how it is considered to be such an outstanding democracy. It has become outstanding recently simply by its dysfunction. The Electoral College is a farce, where a President can still assume office after being defeated by the popular vote of the country's citizens. When the unbridled actions of the President as an administrative officer mirror the rule of a third world dictator, then the country is no longer a democracy. The proof is in the present loss of respect for America by the leaders of the Western World.

Some of the extreme rhetoric coming from the President and from his cronies and his family members is characteristic of the strident adulation of world dictators past and present. One needs only to google the film clips of Hitler rallies in the 1930s to view the frenzy that can be created in a crowd by such unruly cheerleading.

The United States is Canada's nearest neighbour. The two countries share a similar heritage and thus a special relationship. That neighbour, however, can be overpowering in many ways. It is said that when the United States sneezes, Canada catches a cold. The health of our neighbour is therefore a huge concern to Canadians. Right now, the political health of the US is suffering from a raging fever, and it is very worrisome to all of America's international friends and allies. America's long-touted democracy is at a tipping point through the words and actions of a cabal within the Administration. The erosion of American democratic institutions is happening at an alarming rate.

Outside the United States, Canadians and citizens of other nations across the world are able to get access to unadulterated news coverage of current American and world events. Too many Americans though, have only a blinkered view of what is happening in their own country, and they know virtually nothing of life outside their own borders. They have no comprehension of how the far the former respect for their country has fallen in the eyes of the rest of the world.

To those of us watching from a distance, we cannot help being concerned that once the economy falters in the months ahead, the sweeping social protests in the United States will spin out of control and lawlessness will take over. The President and his Administration will consolidate his powers on the excuse of dealing with the disturbances. Disorder could spill over the American borders. The implications are frightening.

It is unnerving that many Americans are obsessed with the ownership of guns. It is frightening to see the glorification of military style guns whose sole purpose is to kill people.

The other huge concern at this time is what the "new normal" will be as a result of the coronavirus. Will there be additional waves of the outbreak? Will there be a vaccine and will it be effective? How long will we be subject to wearing masks and social distancing? Living here in Truro, we have been lucky to be within the "Atlantic Bubble," where the borders have been closed to travellers from the rest of Canada and from all other countries. The Bubble has worked

in restricting the number of cases that could come in from
elsewhere.

It would certainly be welcome to have more freedom to socialize,
but it is better to keep the borders closed in the hopes of staying
healthy until better treatment methods and a safe vaccine are found.
In the meantime, we have an opportunity to learn new habits,
perhaps make lifestyle changes and be more aware of the world
around us.

The future will be challenging, certainly in the next year or two, but
perhaps this experience will lead us to be a more thoughtful and
caring society.

David C. Clark, September 2020

APPENDIX "A"

For the information of the reader I provide the following listing of some of the people that my family and I would have been most familiar with during the war time period.

-Dot/Dorothy (my mother, Dorothy May Clark, housewife and gardener)

-Tallie/Charlie (my father, Charles R. Clark, farmer and carpenter)

-Laurel/Doodles/Siddy (my sister, who would have been 10 years old in July 1938)

-Dr. Lawrence B.W. and Jessie Braine (my grandparents, GP doctor, Annapolis Royal)

-Robert (mother's brother, Rev. Robert Braine, United Church Minister in Trenton, Pictou Co)

- Betty (mother's sister, Elizabeth Braine, Robert & Betty twins, she worked in Newington, Connecticut)

-Anne/Skip and Bill (Auntie Anne Ward, RN, father's sister, Bill engineer at Creamery, son Billy/Wm.)

-Kate (Aunt Kate Norman, RN, father's sister, widow, sons Francis/Leo & Alec, Katherine and Jane)

-Fan and Fenton (Aunt Fan Weatherbie, Barrachois, father's sister, Don, Emma, Anne and Elmer

-Anne /Bridget (Miss Anne Lombard, RN, home from work in New York in July & August)

-Freddie/Freddy (Florence Fredrick, RN, very close friend of Anne Lombard, also visiting from NY)

-Earle (Earle Lombard, bachelor, neighboring farm across the Lake Road)

-Nellie/ Lommy (Mrs. Lombard, mother of Anne and Earle, Bill and Jim)

-Henry and Etta (father's Uncle Henry, farm on Lake Road just west of Slade Road)

-Elwell and Ferne (Clark, father's 1st cousin, Henry's son, moving to Saskatchewan)

-Alec and Melita Clark (father's first cousin, Henry's son, lived with his parents on Lake Road farm)

-Margaret (Margaret Clark, later Dickenson, father's first cousin, Henry and Etta's daughter)

-Jennie and Cecil (Mr. and Mrs. C.G. Fulton, owner CG Fulton Pharmacy, son Junior)

-Janie and Davy (Mr. and Mrs. D.R. Bell, son Raymond, neighbouring farm toward village)

-Warren and Greta (Mr. and Mrs. Warren Bell, neighboring farm closer to village, Greta a teacher)

-Clara and Frank (Mr. and Mrs. Frank Buckler, farm equipment dealer, daughters Janet and Joan)

-Annie and Cecil (Mr. and Mrs. Cecil Langille, he worked at creamery, daughter Jean)

-Frances and Jimmy (Mr. and Mrs. James White, owner of Selrite 5 & 10, Shirley and Terry)

-Hattie and Earl (Mr. and Mrs. Earle Langille, he worked at creamery)

-Maude and Isobel MacLellan (spinster sisters, retired nurse and teacher)

-Hilda and Edna Langille (spinster sisters, Hilda my elementary school teacher)

-Helen and Jimmy (Mr. and Mrs. Jimmy MacKeen, Ford dealership, sons Jon & David, daughter Jean)

-Muriel and Harry (Mr. and Mrs. Harry Bryden, market gardener, son Lloyd, daughter Margaret Anne)

-Hance and Laura Coulter (neighbor ½ mile toward village, son Jack, daughters Loretta & Evelyn)

-Mr. and Mrs. J.J. Creighton, (owner of Tatamagouche Creamery, sons Austin, Ian, Mervyn)

-Mag Patterson (Miss Margaret Patterson, spinster owner of Lynwood Inn)

-Janie and Will Donaldson (son Gordon, neighboring farm French River Bridge)

-George (Donaldson, bachelor, farm just beyond 3rd bridge at Donaldson's)

-Nan and Fred Langille, (Lake Road farm opposite Millbrook Road, Connie and Graham)

-Rhoda and Alvah MacKinnon (Jimmy, Curtis & Parker, Martha, Lulu & Ella, farm up behind Lombards)

-Mrs. Maggie Manthorne (Rhoda's mother who lived with MacKinnons or vice versa)

-Helen and Tip Sproule (forester working in Tatamagouche, son Dale)

-Madge and Jim Langille (he was an insurance agent, lived down behind Main Street)

-Mrs. Crowe (elderly lady who lived across the road from the Buzz Clark/future ACTC)

-Miss Janie Powers (spinster, operated a small millenary shop in village)

- Mr. Longley (Graham Longley, may have been an agriculture rep, later killed in war)

-Hallie (Clark, father's 2nd cousin, bachelor, labourer, lived farm future site of Balmoral Motel)

-Mr. and Mrs Charlie Bryden (lived farm south of future Hills of Annan)

-Aunt Hannah (mother of father's 2nd cousin Lawrence Clark, lived on original Clark homestead)

-Mr. Whidden (Minister, Sharon United, transferred to Cape Breton)

APPENDIX "B"

Brief selected excerpts from daily diaries of Dorothy M. Clark, of Tatamagouche

(Full transcripts on file with Tatamagouche Archives)

1937

May 12 - Mrs. Lombard and I took Frank, the Lombard's horse, and went down to the Coronation Celebration for George VI, at the Town Hall. It was nice. Mr. Whidden, Dr. Murray, Mr. Philpott and Bill Nelson spoke.

Jun 3 – The Duke of Windsor's wedding day.

Jun 29 – Election day. Tallie and I went down town after dinner to vote. Liberals won big majority. Angus L. MacDonald for Premier.

Oct 4 – A shower today for Greta Langille, Laurel's teacher, who is engaged to Warren Bell.

Dec 3 – Kate went during the night as nurse down to Gordon Mattatall's. They had a baby boy.

1938

Jan 19 – Charlie left this AM by train for Halifax to Dairymen's Convention. Francis Norman is here doing the barn work.

Jan 28 – Tallie and I started out after dinner and skated over to Fan's in Barrachois. Ice good.

Feb 24 - Aunt Hannah Clark died through the night. Charlie and Earle went up to the Clark Cemetery this afternoon to dig the grave.

Oct 1 – (Laurel writing) – Mum took castor oil this morning. After dinner Mum said it was coming so we got ready and went to Middleton hospital. Got there about 15 past 2. Baby was born at 7 past 4. The baby was a boy. Called it David Charles Braine Clark. Weighed 8 lbs 7 ½ oz.

Dec 18 - Jimmy MacKeen's had a baby son – David Alexander.

1939

Mar 26 – Muriel and Harry Bryden had a baby girl this afternoon, Margaret Ann.

Apr 28 – Today Hitler's Reichstag speech replying to Roosevelt.

May 21 – Listened on radio to MacKenzie King speak from Ottawa.

Aug 14 – Hallie Weatherbie, Fenton and Fan's son, was drowned off their wharf at 5 this PM.

Sep 1 – War. Hitler invaded Poland at dawn this morning.

Sep 3 – Britain and France declared war on Germany this AM.

Sep 4 – War news on radio all the time. So depressing.

Sep 10 – Canada declared war on Germany.

Sep 27 – We hear such conflicting reports on radio as to war. It's hard to know what is what.

Oct 26 - Kate went to Springhill hospital with Doug Halverson's. They had twin boys, Kenneth and Keith.

Nov 23 – Had a meeting here in evening to try to form a Credit Union. Earle Lombard, George Donaldson, Fred Langille, Doug Cunningham and Mr. Longley here. Late when they left.

Nov 28 – News bad tonight. Russia and Finland will get in it I think.

1940

Jan 13 – Junior Fulton sick with asthma. Very miserable.

Jan 20 – Charlie has been appointed Clerk of Works on the new post office.

Jan 30 – Mrs. Lombard called to say that schools are to be closed for two weeks on account of measles.

Mar 27 – Such a sweeping victory as Liberals had. Of course we're pleased on account of Tallie's job. Had Credit Union here at night. Just Nan and Fred, Janie Donaldson, George and Earle.

Apr 9 – Germany invaded Norway and Denmark today. Listen to news every chance we get.

Apr 17 – Junior Fulton died this morning. Everyone feels terrible.

Apr 19 – Funeral this afternoon at two in the church. Tallie took the car and Earle and I went down. The school children marched. Heaps and heaps of flowers.

May 25 – We got home to find that Tallie had been idle all day as all Public Works are closed on account of war.

Jun 6 – A terrible thunder storm overnight. Went to town in AM to hear that Fenton Weatherbie's barn had been struck and burned. Six horses and two calves killed. Tallie went down and was gone all day fixing up a place for the cows. It was an awful storm all over the Maritimes.

Jul 25 – Got yarn to knit a sweater for the Red Cross.

Aug 21 – Got up early and took flowers down. I exhibited asters, snapdragons, stocks and petunias. Got prizes on the asters and stocks. Flower Show lovely.

Aug 28 - Mr. Creighton very sick - was operated on.

Sep 17 – The storm was terrific. About ½ the crop of apples in the Annapolis Valley were blown off. Still rain today but wind abating.

Sep 19 – We went down to see the new Selrite store which opened today.

Oct 10 – Busy getting ready for company. Laurel's teachers arrived at 4:45 and left at nine. Tallie took them down. Both Miss MacFedridge and Miss McDonald nice.

Nov 16 – Went to town. Sold 12 cabbages for a dollar.

Dec 11 – Tallie went down with Earle's truck to get buttermilk. Lauder Perrin's have baby daughter and Arthur Ross's a son. Mrs. John Simpson dead – funeral Friday.

Dec 12 – Charlie and Earle took barley to Balmoral Mill to get smashed. We got 35 pounds of ground oatmeal.

Dec 19 – The Christmas concert. One of the very best concerts. Admission only 15 cents. Ken Bryden so good as Scrooge. Alex MacKay got married tonight.

1941

Jan 12 – Davy Bell ploughed the Lake road this afternoon. Earle and Tallie shovelled.

Feb 6 – Men had to shovel all morning to open road. Tallie had to go to the river for water. I joined W.M.S. and had a good time.

Apr 6 – Germany invaded Greece and Yugoslavia today.

Jun 4 – They had a Field Day and Music Festival at the school. A lovely day for it. Nellie went with me. It was nice but too long.

Jun 13 – Got paid for lumber this AM from Hayman Bros. Charlie bought a share in the tractor.

Jun 15 – Went to church - had special music and the choir wore new gowns for first.

Jun 22 – Germany invaded Russia this morning. We listened to Churchill on radio.

Jun 25 – We got an Electrolux today. Mr. Campbell was around again today so I got one. Tallie was away but I made the necessary arrangements.

Jul 2 – Harry Bonnyman's wedding today.

Aug 14 –We had a chimney fire. Earle came over. We went down town later. Lots of soldiers around. P.C. is feeding 150 at the hall this PM.

Aug 29 – Ben Langille died last night of a heart attack. Tallie and I went down in the evening and took flowers.

Sep 28 – No church on account of scarlet fever.

Oct 8 – I went down town in AM and got the Family Herald. I got 75 cents for prize in contest.

Oct 20 – Greta was up to call for jelly for the Truro Hospital.

Oct 28 – We went down to vote. The Liberals went in with a sweeping majority – 23 seats, Tories 5, and C.C.F. 2.

Dec 3 – Tallie was at Whidden's helping Davy load his truck with their furniture for their move to Cape Breton.

Dec 7 – Japan declared war on U.S. and Great Britain today. What will it all mean as there are no nations left out this time except South America?

Dec 8 – Great Britain declared war on Japan today.

Dec 19 – Laurel down in AM for tree at school. She got a mirror, comb and case from Ken Bryden. Charlie and I down to the church at night when they presented Mr. Whidden with a purse of $137. Big crowd there.

1942

Jan – Lois McKay of Stellarton and Ian Creighton were married this afternoon at 3 o'clock.

Jan 27 - Sugar is rationed to ¾ pound per person per week. We were lucky having bought a bag about two weeks ago.

Jan 31 – It is fine at last. They started to shovel the road about 9:30AM and didn't finish until after 4 PM. Davy and Warren brought the truck and they ploughed and the others kept shoveling. It is just like a tunnel between the Wilson Creek bridge and Davy's.

Feb 5 – Went down to card party in the hall. It was for Russian War Relief. Had a good time.

Feb 9 – We went on Daylight Saving time today.

Mar 17 - The Sproules have a boy, Dale, born today and the Carson Murray's another one.

Mar 27 - Janie called up about eight PM and asked if we were going to be home and I didn't catch on. About nine o'clock Davy and Janie, Hance and Laura, Greta and Warren, Frank and Clara, and Earle came to celebrate our 15th wedding anniversary. They were all dressed up in the craziest costumes. Had a lunch along and did they ever take us by surprise. Davy and Janie gave us two glasses, C & F 2 pitchers, Hance and Laura the cutest salt and peppers, and Greta and Warren a measuring cup. The anniversary was supposed to be glass. We had a grand time.

Apr 5 - David has another cold in his nose and we gave him castor oil again.

Apr 16 - Went down to the church service at night. Mr Davis induction as Minister today. It was terrible. A Dr. Betts was there and he was so dramatic I laughed so hard I got hysterical. Had a nice social afterward. Mr. Davis has a nice face, so friendly and she looks sensible but scared to death.

May 1 - A Bonnell boy got caught in a saw mill and had a hand taken off and two legs badly cut. They think they will have to be amputated. They don't expect him to live.

May 23 - Jane, Laurel and I went down to the wedding in the church. Ethel Murray married Burt Livingstone at 4:30 PM. We went down about 3:30 and got a great seat up in the gallery. A very pretty bride and wedding. She was in white, Betty [Murray] was in green and Dawn in pink.

May 28 - We are rationed to ½ pound sugar per person per week and ½ usual tea and ¼ coffee.

Jun 7 - We went down to Freddie Weatherbie's in AM for live lobsters and got 19 for $1.00

Aug 22 – Charlie went with me in the morning and we took down 6 dozen ears of corn. I sold them to MacQueens's market for 25 cents a dozen.

Oct 21 – The Red Cross of Tata fed 180 soldiers to-day so asked us to make pies and biscuits.

Dec 24 - We had a nice quiet evening together. Listened to "Henry Aldrich" on the radio.

1943

Jan 6 – Jim Langille had one leg amputated today.

Jan 21 - There was to be a bridge party tonight to aid Russia, but we didn't go.

Mar 11 –There's a lot of controversy over Mr. Davis' sermon last Sunday in which he condemned the movies, raffling quilts, etc.

Mar 30 – Had woodsaw today so had to hustle around and make drop cookies, cream pie, scones and baked beans. Just had seven men for meal. They finished at 5:30PM.

Apr 3 – The Norman boys, Francis and Alex, have both been called to enlist in military.

Apr 22 – Francis brought up some smelts at dinnertime. Harry Bryden here until ten in the evening – he was supposed to be patrolling the river for people poaching smelts

May 27 – Went in to Isobel Byers' shop trying on dresses and looked at a seersucker for Laurel but she wanted $5.95 for them so I'll hold off for a while.

Jun 9 - Carl O'Neil and Florence Cole were married tonight

Jun 13 – I went to church while Tallie, Laurel and David. Went to Freddie Weatherbie's and got 11 lb of lobsters for a dollar. I wore my new hat and Jennie wore hers. William Ward, Jr. came home last night on 10 days leave from the army.

Jul 6 – Jennie and I got bawled out on the telephone for talking so much tying up party line.

Jul 18 – Greta and I went to church. Clifford Stewart, a student, preached who gave us a real gospel sermon. Earle has a hired man, Geordie Swan – 15 years old.

Aug 18 – Got ready to go to Westchester. I made sandwiches and then took my stuff down to exhibit at the Flower Show. We got away in Earle's truck after dinner. Such lovely blueberries that we found. Kate and the girls, Mrs. Manthorne, Nellie, Anne and Earle, Charlie, Laurel, David and I went. We got two buckets full picking by hand.

Aug 28 – Had to go down town in the AM to get new ration books.

Sep 30 – Harry Bonnyman's have a son "Jimmy".

Oct 1 – David's 5th birthday. I made a cake right after breakfast and Frank and Clara came bringing him two bantam hens and a rooster, and a bouquet of flowers.

Oct 20 – Bill Ward came up about 9AM to start the wiring of the barn.

Nov 2 – Got 1 ½ lbs sugar – not much but I'm grateful for that.

Dec 4 – I couldn't cook any on account of not having any sugar due to rationing.

Dec 22 – Laurel went to Wallace Station on the morning train with Jane to see Katherine. Charlie went down at 9:30 PM for her, but the train didn't get here until eleven. They ran out of gas and had to get some from Smith MacPherson.

Dec 25 - We had the bantams for Christmas dinner.

1944

Feb 4 - Laurel came home from school before dinner. Mr. Hamilton is giving up teaching and Mrs. R.B. Fraser is to take over Monday, for a while anyway.

Feb 6 – Raining at last. We need the water for the tank in the cellar.

Feb 29 - Made 2 cakes and 2 lots of brownies and frosted them. Also pineapple squares. Jennie came up about 3 PM and we made sandwiches and she made frosting. Had a six table bridge party and sleigh ride. Tallie went down for them with the team and bobsled and they got here about 8 o'clock. They all seemed to enjoy it. Helen MacKeen got 1st prize, Virginia 2nd, and Frances and Clara travelling prizes. Had Janie, Greta, Clara, Sue MacBurnie, Annie, Florence Dewar, Margaret MacL, Marion, Mrs. Ells Langille, Verna, Anne W, Betty Murray, Alice, Lou Wilson, Marie, Isobel B, Helen MacK, Mrs. Creighton, Muriel, Jennie, Fan, Virginia Perrin, Mrs Lutes, Florence Forbes. Asked Jean Langille at bank, Mrs R.B. Fraser, Helen Bonnyman, but they didn't come. Frances was away. Kate, Hattie and Laura Coulter came but not to play.

Mar 5 - The men all turned out in the PM and are opening up the road after the blizzard.

May 26 - Alvah MacKinnons got word today that Parker is seriously wounded.

Jun 3 - Kenny Langille married Ruth Tattrie today.

Jun 19 - Don Ross got back from his honeymoon today so Charlie and I went down in the evening to the banjo. He seems happy and she's not bad looking.

Jul 11 - Charlie took the children and me down to the auction sale at Buzz Clark's. I bid 50 cents of a Cornflower vase, 3 plates and a pitcher, and I got them.

Nov 23 - Johnny Bonnyman found dead in barn today.

1945

Jan 20 - Wards got a cable from William that he has arrived in England safely.

Feb 2 - I made a pair of pillow cases out of the feed bags to match the bedspread.

Feb 15 - Today is sugar day at the store but didn't get to town and I am all cleaned out.

Apr 12 - Roosevelt died today of a cerebral hemorrhage. World shocked.

Apr 18 - Jennie called to say Rolly Langille had been released by Americans.

Apr 29 - Mussolini executed in Milan today.

May 1 - Hitler died today as reports go.

May 4 - Had a letter from William. He is at present in Holland.

May 7 - Jennie called to say the war in Europe is over. VE Day will be tomorrow. Tuesday and Wednesday to be holidays.

May 8 - Tuesday - Today will be VE Day, which will be a great day - to go down in history. We went down to the church to the 11 o'clock service. Church was packed. We had a bonfire later.

Jun 10 - Laurel and I went to church. The 20th anniversary of church union. A big turn out.

Jun 24 - Emma Weatherbie has her diamond from Harry Matheson.

Jun 28 - Went to Betty Murray's operetta last night. It was marvellous.

Oct 25 - I voted. The Liberals went in again. 28 Liberals and 2 CCF. No Tories.

Nov 1 - I washed and bleached 13 feed bags. I want to make some curtains for Mother.

Nov 13 - Mrs R.B. Fraser and Mrs. Whidden tackled me about being secretary of the W.M.S., which I ended up saying I would.

Dec 13 - Charlie making wooden guns for the costumes for the school Christmas concert.

1946

Jan 3 - I went to see Hilda Langille about David not going to school.

Feb 2 - Used my new pressure cooker for the first time and was so afraid it would explode.

Feb 3 - Mr. Davis preached another one of his sermons to waken people up. I don't feel any different toward him though.

Feb 12 - Tommy Simpson here for both dinner and supper. I am very happy to be getting the water in. Men worked until 2 AM getting the taps in. What a thrill at last.

Feb 17 - Jennie says Mrs. Davis is having a neighbourly tea tomorrow. Well let her have it - I'd hate to accept anyway.

Feb 26 - Made pair of pajamas for David from feedbags

Mar 1 - Went down to Johnny Ferguson's in AM for 11 young pigs.

Mar 17 - Went to church. It was the dedication of the new organ. It was lovely.

Mar 20 - There was a reception at the hall for returned boys tonight so I made cupcakes in the afternoon. Went to hall at night to serve. William Ward made a speech.

Mar 21 - Boiling sap all day.

Apr 1 - David started back to school today.

Apr 11 - Our ham is just about done. That pig lasted quite a while.

Apr 28 - Mr. Davis preached a personal sermon about pensions which I hate.

May 4 - Went down and delivered my eggs and took Jennie her cream. Sold seven doz eggs.

May 9 - Went down at night and got David a cat from Allison Reid. Hideous, but he loves it.

Jun 8 - Drove the horses while Charlie sowed fertilizer with the lime spreader.

Jun 19 - David and I went out the Four Pound Road for Ladies' Slippers and found quite a few.

Jun 24 - Belle the horse has colic and we had to get the vet. Hope she will be alright.

Jun 25 - Made cake and cupcakes for shower for Melita Weatherbie, engaged to Alex Clark. Laurel and Janie went with me. She got nice gifts.

Aug 3 - Jim Langille here to sell life insurance for David.

Aug 7 - We all went up to the Six Mile Brook for a picnic.

Aug 31 - Made a pie, then went down to Ward's to get Charlie's sister Laura and Ted. Went down to the river in the PM for a swim. Charlie started to bind grain and Ted helped. Enjoyed having them so much.

Sep 17 - Emma Weatherbie's wedding day.

Sep 28 - Got away for the VG nurse's residence about 8AM. Felt badly leaving Laurel for everything was so strange to her. It was a tiring trip.

Oct 1 - We gave David 2 muskrat traps for his birthday.

Oct 22 - I brought in 50 cabbages from the garden.

Nov 11 - We all went down for the Memorial Service in the church.

Nov 18 - Mrs. Lockerby called to say Laurel and Margaret are coming on the bus to Truro and could we meet them.

Dec 23 - Churned so we could give Mother and Dad some butter to take home with them. Made 21 pounds and it is nice.

Dec 25 - I miss Laurel but I imagine she is lonesome too. Our first Christmas without her.

Dec 26 - Selrite store burned this afternoon. David and I went down to see the fire. Don't see how they contained it.

Dec 31 - Frances took us into the store. Such a wreck. She is feeling so badly and we will miss it so much. I took her some butter.

Hard Times, by David C. Clark

CREDITS

Some of the general information included in this narrative has been gleaned from the following sources:

-Bonnyman, Allan C. - The Cookhouse - 2015

-Campbell, Ron – Personal email correspondence - 2020

-Clark, Dorothy M. - Personal Diary – 1937 to 1942

-Crawford, Sybil Henderson - Personal email correspondence - 2020

-Johnson. Anne G. – <u>Grahams and Braines</u> - 2012

-Kennedy, Roy - <u>Each in Turn</u> – 1980

-Norman, Dr. Jane & Morton, Barbara – The <u>Clarks of Insch, Scotland and Tatamagouche, Nova Scotia</u> – 1981

-Patterson, Frank H., <u>Acadian Tatamagouche and Fort Franklin</u> - 1947

-Patterson, Frank H., <u>History of Tatamagouche</u> – 1973

-Whiston. Norris M., <u>Cobequid Meguma and Acadian Villages</u> -2016

-White, Terry - Personal email correspondence - 2020

PHOTOS

To see a few photos related to this publication, visit:

www.davidclark.ca/hardtimes

ABOUT THE AUTHOR - DAVID C. CLARK

David Charles Braine Clark was born in the old Soldiers' Memorial Hospital in Middleton, Annapolis County, Nova Scotia, on October 1st, 1938. The reason for the Middleton location was due to his grandfather who assisted in the delivery having been a family practice medical doctor in Annapolis Royal, and having his hospital privileges in Middleton. Dave spent all his early life from one week to eighteen years of age growing up in Tatamagouche.

David C. Clark has been a professional land surveyor for more than fifty-eight years. He is licensed to practice in Nova Scotia and the State of Maine, and has worked on surveying projects in five Canadian Provinces. Dave is a Past President and Life Member of the Association of Nova Scotia Land Surveyors and a Past President of the 3,000 member Canadian Council of Land Surveyors.

Dave's working career spanned 39 years with the Canada Cement Company and Lafarge Corporation, located in Brookfield, Nova Scotia and Havelock, New Brunswick. Over the years he has worked as a construction inspector, blaster, heavy construction equipment operator, mineral prospector, wilderness guide, and for a greater part of his career as a manager in heavy industry.

Dave has been married to Deanna (Greene) for 55 years. They have two children, Jonathan and Anne (McDonah), and four grandchildren, Evan, Alex, Sarah and Olivia McDonah.

Dave enjoys writing in his spare time. For a number of years he wrote technical articles for publication in Canadian and American professional magazines, and in newspapers, before switching to fiction. He has three other published books in paperback and eBook formats, two being fiction and the third an anthology of some of his land surveying experiences in short story format. One of Dave's books, *Ingonish Dilemma*, received first prize in the contemporary romance fiction contest of the Toronto chapter of the Romance Writers of America. Dave's works of fiction reflect an inherent familiarity with the people and setting of the Nova Scotia Scottish culture.

Website: www.davidclark.ca

Manufactured by Amazon.ca
Bolton, ON